About the author

Just one visit to the ice rink was all it took for Nicola to *fall* for ice skating. Aged 11, she promptly hung up her ballet shoes to skate, skate, skate in every spare moment she could find. What a fantastic discovery it was ... a perfect combination of fun and challenges had been found!

Not a minute was lost in trying to master moves from forward crossovers to mohawks. The ballet exams and performances, meanwhile, remained *on ice* although some elements began to appear on the rink. To this day, Nicola can't resist adding the odd arabesque to her repertoire. It's a great escape from the desk at home where she works writing children's books.

Just one *trip* was all it took for Nicola to fall and break her ankle! With a foot *in ice* awaiting plaster and skates gathering dust, Nicola was thrilled to be asked to write this book. It is dedicated to her daughters, Sophie and Helena, and their Australian cousin, Isabella.

3

Introduction

Do you love to watch the athletic and graceful displays of ice skating championships from the comfort of your sofa? Do you wonder what it takes to perform such amazing  feats? You are not alone! Ice skating attracts record numbers of television viewers during the championships. From the spectacular jumps of figure skating, through the drama and intricate footwork of ice dance, to the thrill of speed skating – it's an exciting and varied world.

But you don't have to compete at Olympic level to enjoy ice skating as a great form of exercise, relaxation and fun. While one skater's dream may be to perform the ultimate triple Axel jump, another's may be to skate a few circuits of the rink with friends. Ice skating is a very sociable sport and you'll never be short of a super.activ challenge.

Whether you're an absolute beginner or a skater wanting to improve technique, this book will carefully guide you through the basic moves, turns, and jumps. We've included plenty of useful tips and, because the world of ice skating is so fascinating, you'll find some interesting historical and awe-inspiring facts too.

So enjoy reading, make a date with the ice rink and *put your skates on!*

Nicola

4

super.activ

ICE SKATING

Nicola Hall

Illustrated by Sally Launder

Consultant: Peter Morrissey
The National Ice Skating Association of
the UK Limited

*Hodder
Children's
Books*

a division of Hodder Headline Limited

For Sophie, Helena and Isabella. Happy skating!

The author would like to give special thanks to Dennis L. Bird, Archivist and Historian, The National Ice Skating Association (NISA) of UK Limited.

Text copyright 2000 © Nicola Hall
Illustrations copyright 2000 © Sally Launder
Published by Hodder Children's Books 2000

Series design by Fiona Webb
Book design by Don Martin
Edited by Caroline Plaisted

10 9 8 7 6 5 4 3 2 1

A catalogue record for this book is available from the British Library.

ISBN 0 340 73981 9

Printed by Clays Ltd, St Ives plc

Hodder Children's Books
a division of Hodder Headline Limited
338 Euston Road
London NW2 3BH

Contents

Look it up!

If you come across a word or term that you don't recognise, look it up in the glossary on page 124.

1 How it all began

first skates • the Dutch • the British • the Americans • first champions

Watching the dazzling performances of today's stars, or skating to the latest music at your local rink, it's difficult to imagine how ice skating first started.

Archaeologists believe skating began during northern Europe's harsh winters over one thousand years ago. In those days skating was a means of survival – after all, some way of crossing the frozen rivers and lakes simply had to be found. Lunch may have depended on it! Style, glamour and sequins were not major concerns; but getting somewhere and staying upright were!

Sticks and bones – the first skates

The earliest skates were probably made from sharpened oxen or reindeer bones and would have been bound to the feet with leather. But, no matter how sharp the rib- or shin-bones were, they could not cut into and grip the ice sufficiently. Progress would have been slow.

A hand-held, long stick was the answer to the early skater's difficulties. Using one with a spiked end – as you would use a ski pole today – enabled skaters to push themselves forwards and stay upright. With this simple equipment, people could now skate quickly across frozen rivers and lakes rather than travel the long distances around the outside.

This 10th century Viking boot skate is an example of what experts believe to be one of the first skates.

7

The skating evolution

Over time people looked for new ways to improve the first
skates. The materials used became more effective,
supportive and comfortable, and new skating techniques
gradually developed.

The Netherlands – from work to leisure

During the 14th and 16th centuries, much of the
Netherlands' trading took place on or alongside its many
waterways. The icy winters of the time, however, could
have delayed business.

Ice skating was the solution to the winter problem and it
also became a popular pastime. Skates allowed traders to
use the icy stretches as roadways for their goods. Impressed
onlookers, meanwhile, began to join them on the ice just
for fun.

Ironmasters

All this interest encouraged the Dutch to redesign the iron
skates that had first appeared in Iceland some years earlier.
The resulting skates – finished in the late 1500s – were
heavy but they could carve and grip the ice quite successfully. Sticks and poles were thrown away! Unlike the skates
before them, these shaped ones didn't slip on the ice.

Sport of kings (-to-be)

By the 17th century, canal racing on wooden skates with iron blades was popular amongst the Dutch. It only took a winter in exile in the Netherlands for James – younger son of the British monarch Charles I – to fall for the sport. On his arrival home in 1662, James, Duke of York was excited to find that England's rivers had also frozen! No time was lost in introducing this 'new' sport to the British aristocracy.

18th Century go-fast skates!

Keen to reach ever faster speeds on the ice, the Dutch created skates with longer blades.

The British influence

THE SKATING TIMES
December 1750

Watch out Holland! Skates to cut a figure!

Speed skating – the popular ice sport of Holland – has recently hit the headlines with the new, Dutch-designed speed skate. English skate makers meanwhile are ready to unveil the first figure skate. Tests show that figures – tracings of the figure eight and additional circles and loops – can be performed with some accuracy in the new skate.

The revolutionary feature of the figure skate is the grooved, curved blade that extends beyond the heel. With its ability to take the effort out of turns, the skate's excited creators believe it could lead to a booming interest in figure skating. Just how many people can afford such a skate remains to be seen.

The new skates attract attention from skaters at trials in London.

What's the figure?

Figure skating tested a skater's control and balance but demanded lots of practice, patience and time: figure eights, three-circle figures and loops had to be traced on the ice in perfect patterns. It remained the sport of the aristocracy for only they – being short of neither time nor money – could afford the very expensive lessons!

The English style of figure skating began towards the end of the 18th century. Unlike the International style seen on the television today, where the skater is continually moving position, the English style involved holding graceful positions until a turn or change of direction. Skaters kept an upright posture with arms often held at their sides. Great concentration was on the figures being traced on the ice.

11

A style fit for a queen

The English style was *the* style by the time of Queen Victoria of England's coronation in 1837. With its strict rules and controlled manner, it fitted the Victorian times perfectly. Queen Victoria and Prince Albert both owned the most impressive pairs of made-to-measure skates. Records suggest, however, that it was Prince Albert who loved the sport.

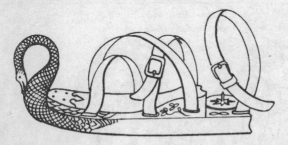

Prince Albert's skate from 1851: notice the decorative metal blade in the shape of a swan.

Queen Victoria's skate was made in 1854. The full, leather shoe is very detailed and is attached to a wooden sole. Compare it with the simple skate below.

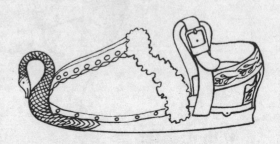

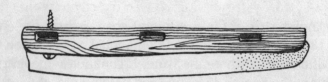

An English skate from 1850, with a wooden sole and a metal blade that extends as far as the heel. Unlike earlier skates that were simply strapped on, this one would have been screwed to the boot as well.

The American dream ...

... to *steel* the show ...

In 1850, the first steel skate was produced in America. Once sharpened, steel blades gripped the ice like no other blade before them. They were also strong and lighter than iron. Suddenly it became possible for skaters to perform previously tricky moves.

... skate *on the edge!*

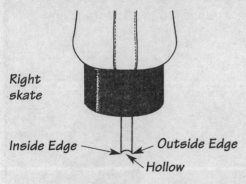

Right skate

Inside Edge —— Outside Edge

Hollow

The steel blade improved even further when the Americans formed a hollow along its length. This created the 'inside' and 'outside' edges you see on today's skates.

... with greater control *to boot!*

Special skating boots soon followed and the new steel skates could be clamped or screwed directly to them. With the boots laced up tightly to secure and support the foot, and the skates firmly attached, skaters found they had even more control over their movements. Figure skating began to change ...

Star profile – Jackson Haines (USA)

The world of figure skating was turned around when Jackson Haines entered the scene wearing the 'new', improved-performance skates. Born in 1840 in Chicago, Haines had trained as a ballet dancer. Not for him the stiff and feet-focused obsession of English-style skating that was popular in America: Haines loved to skate to music, and set out to bring the graceful and expressive movement of ballet to the ice! His free movement of arms, legs, head and body initially shocked the Victorian followers of the English style. But his free-style skating had a theatrical quality that the Austrians, Germans, Russians, Hungarians and Swedes adored. Before long, Haines' popularity extended to the Americans and British, and skaters began to copy his style.

Haines created moves such as the spiral and sit spin that you will see skaters perform today. Jackson Haines died in his mid-thirties in 1875. His gravestone lies in Finland with the words, 'The American Skating King'. Today Haines is remembered as the pioneer of modern skating who brought music and a freer 'Internatonal' style to the skating world.

Competitions – gamblers lead the way forward!

Figure skating in England remained a pastime of the wealthy into the early 19th century and beyond. Speed skating on the icy Cambridgeshire fens, however, had become a popular sport for gamblers, skaters, and farm labourers alike. But heavy betting and dubious race results ended in many a heated dispute!

A local Journalist, James Drake Digby, saw an urgent need for proper rules and fixed distances for all championships. In 1879, he founded the National Skating Association (NSA), now called the National Ice Skating Association (NISA) of the UK. Skating associations soon formed around the world, the rules became similar, and figure skating joined ranks.

Today you will find national ice skating associations in most countries around the world. They are a good starting point for enquiries about the sport in your country.

DID YOU KNOW?
Speed skating and figure skating became two of the first sports to compete at international level following the formation of the International Skating Union (ISU) in 1892. Today, the ISU oversees all major international ice skating competitions and championships.

Skating sensation!

In 1902, in the absence of a separate women's competition, Mrs Florence Madeleine Syers of Great Britain competed in the first Men's World Figure Skating Championships and nearly won! Madge Syers (as she was known) was awarded the Silver Medal, while the Gold was won by the legendary Ulrich Salchow of Sweden.

Madge Syers had focused attention on women skaters but, in 1903, the International Skating Union (ISU) banned women from entering the men's competitions again. The fashion of the time had been long, bulky dresses and the ISU argued that you couldn't see a woman's footwork in them.

The first Women's World Figure Skating Championships were held at a separate venue to the Men's in 1906 and Mrs Syers won the Gold Medal outright. With her husband, Edgar, she also won the Bronze Medal at the first World Pairs Skating Championships in 1908. She died after childbirth in 1917 at the age of 35.

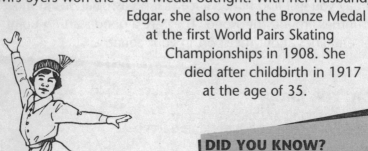

DID YOU KNOW?
Between 1901 and 1905, and between 1907 and 1911, Ulrich Salchow won 10 World Figure Skating titles – the world record for the most Men's Singles titles.

Going for gold ... and glamour!

Sonja Henie was born in Oslo, Norway, in 1912. In 1928, aged 15 years and 315 days, she became the youngest figure skater to have won an Olympic Gold Medal. (This record was broken in 1998 by Tara Lipinski (USA), aged 15 years and 255 days.) Between 1927 and 1936 Sonja won all ten of the Women's World Championship titles – an existing women's world record.

But Sonja was not just a champion skater. She was an individual who captivated her audiences with her style. While other female skaters wore the long and cumbersome skirts of the time, Sonja Henie performed jumps, spins and ballet-like moves in knee-length skirts. When other female skaters were wearing the same black skating boots as men, Sonja wore beige. As soon as beige boots became popular, she changed to white!

Sonja Henie's dazzling charm led to her appearance in 13 films and made her a Hollywood star. As the first celebrity ice skater, her fame brought figure skating to a wider audience. Sonja Henie died in 1969, having changed the world of women's figure skating forever.

Skating firsts – World Championships

1880	British Speed Skating Championships
1893	Men's World Speed Skating Championships
1896	Men's World Figure Skating Championships
1906	Women's World Figure Skating Championships
1908	World Pairs Skating Championships
1936	Women's World Speed Skating Championships
1952	World Ice Dancing Championships

Starting points

rinks • sessions • lessons • clothes

In the 21st century you won't be restricted to skating during icy winters, nor will you have to brave the elements. In Australia you can skate on the hottest of summer days at any one of the country's 18 indoor ice rinks!

Finding an ice rink

Wherever you are in the world, you almost certainly live within relatively easy reach of an ice rink. If you've not yet discovered yours, try contacting one of the ice skating associations on pages 122-123. Once you've decided which rink you're going to, it's a good idea to phone before your visit to check the times of the different sessions.

Ice hockey! I thought the ice disco started at 8.15...

DID YOU KNOW?

1860   The first covered rink was created in Canada –
a large shed over natural ice!

1876   The first indoor rink with artificially frozen ice
opened in London, England. Its creator, Professor
John Gamgee, had some years earlier been looking
for a means of freezing meat for the long journey
from Australia. He invented a method for making
artificial ice and set up an ice-making plant in
Chelsea, London. The first artificial ice rink, or
'Glaciarium', was created on this site.

Sessions and coaching

Just like swimming pools and sports halls, ice rinks have
timetables for all the different sessions they run. There are
general skating sessions that anyone can go along to, and
group coaching for specific abilities. You can join a
beginners' class or – if you've skated before – one for the
next level. Most people start skating in group classes and
then progress to one-
to-one coaching with
a fully qualified
skating coach.

Once you are
confident on the ice,
there are ice discos,
ice dance sessions,
competitions, and
lots more lessons to
choose from.

Will I need coaching?

Coaching is important for learning good skating technique. As a beginner you will be taught such essentials as how to stop and make turns. Coaching is also a great way to boost your ability and confidence on the ice.

Group coaching sessions are a sociable and fun way to learn. They also make you realise that you aren't the only one having a problem learning to stop! In the UK look out for the NISA tesa 'Fun Skate' classes or in Australia the 'Aussie Skate Program'.

What if I'm an in-line skater?

If you're a keen in-line skater, you'll learn quickly. But ice lessons are, however, still a good idea. While many of the basic turns and moves are similar to in-line skating, learning to stop is different. You will also need to learn control of the edges of the blade – something an in-line skate does not have.

How do I choose a class though?

By following these guidelines:

✴ Find a class for a time that you can make without having to rush. You will need to allow half an hour before the lesson to be fitted with hire skates and to warm up.

✴ Ask if you can watch a class before enrolling.

✴ Make sure the coach is qualified and that the class isn't too crowded – you'll need some individual attention.

✴ Check the coach's attention is divided evenly amongst the group. If the pupils look bored, then it's probably the coach that's boring them!

✴ Whether or not he or she has been a champion skater is unimportant when selecting a coach. What is important though is a coach who can explain moves clearly and correct mistakes quickly.

Do I need to take anything to the session?

Pack a kit bag with the following:

✴ an extra sweater.

✴ a spare pair of gloves.

✴ a dense washing-up sponge (about 1cm thick) to cut up as padding for uncomfortable boots.

✴ a small pair of scissors (to cut up the sponge!).

✴ a cloth to dry your blades.

✴ a spare set of laces (only bring these if you have your own boots).

✴ skate guards – to protect blades when not in use.

What should I wear?

You don't need special clothing to go ice skating – a sweatshirt worn with leggings or tracksuit trousers is ideal.

Top tips

* Dress for warmth, wearing layers of clothing. You may feel cold at first, while wanting to take off a layer later.
* Try to wear something with a good-sized pocket. You'll need somewhere to put your locker key and money.
* Dress for comfort. Clothes made from stretchy fabric allow you to move freely. Tight jeans are out!
* Dress for protection. Gloves are essential. Knee and elbow pads are optional.
* Avoid wide trousers, long skirts or scarves. These may get caught up in your skates.
* Wear thin socks or tights – not thick. One pair is all you need.
* Tie up long hair. You want to see where you are going!

What do seasoned skaters wear?

Once experienced, girls may choose to wear simple, short skirts or dresses designed for skating. Boys usually wear a stretch top and trousers (with elastic stirrups to fasten under the boots). Elaborate costumes are for top skaters in competitions!

THE GOLDEN RULES OF THE RINK

Learn these before you hit the ice!

* Skate anti-clockwise only.
* Beginners keep to the outside of the rink.
* Watch where you are going.
* Look behind before you stop and when practising backward moves.
* Don't wear headphones – you need to be aware of other skaters around you!
* Wear gloves for extra protection.
* Always respect the ice rink's own rules on skating etiquette.

Focus on skates

figure skates • ice hockey skates • speed skates • choosing skates • maintaining skates

When people talk about ice skates, they generally mean the boots and blades as a whole. There are three basic types of skate – designed with different features for different techniques – figure skates, ice hockey skates and speed skates. For experienced figure skaters there are also ice dance blades and free-style blades. Most people, however, learn to skate using figure skates.

Figure skating boot (right)

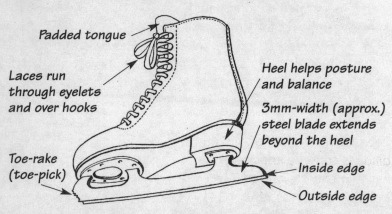

Padded tongue

Laces run through eyelets and over hooks

Toe-rake (toe-pick)

Heel helps posture and balance

3mm-width (approx.) steel blade extends beyond the heel

Inside edge

Outside edge

IT'S BLACK AND WHITE ... USUALLY!
Boys mostly wear black figure skates, while girls wear white. The choice is yours!

The boot is made up of several layers of leather, reinforced at the heel and instep. A good boot should support the ankle well once the boot is laced up.

The toe-rake (toe-pick)

Figure skating blades are usually screwed to the boot and each has a unique teeth-like toe-rake (toe-pick) at the front. These are for performing advanced moves such as spins, toe steps and toe jumps. Unless clowning or stunt performing is your thing, please don't try using toe-rakes as brakes!

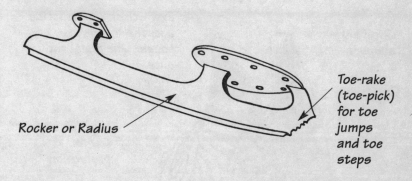

Rocker or Radius

Toe-rake (toe-pick) for toe jumps and toe steps

Edges

The bottom of the figure skate blade is concave and therefore has two edges – one on the inside (next to the other foot): the inside edge, and one on the outside (away from the other foot): the outside edge. Edges must be sharpened or ground regularly to keep a grip on the ice. There's more about this on page 40.

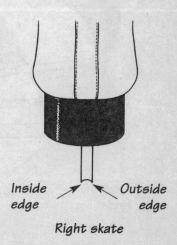

Inside edge   *Outside edge*

Right skate

25

Could you *puck* up the courage?

Ice hockey is the fastest team game in the world. Players wear special, protective gear, and skate with great speed to chase the puck (a flattened rubber disk) and score goals. Once hit with a hockey stick, the puck can travel at amazing speeds of over 150 kilometres per hour. Fast reactions are essential – as are specially designed ice hockey skates like these:

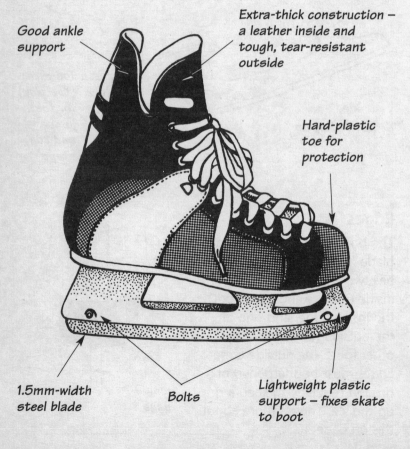

Good ankle support

Extra-thick construction – a leather inside and tough, tear-resistant outside

Hard-plastic toe for protection

1.5mm-width steel blade

Bolts

Lightweight plastic support – fixes skate to boot

ICE HOCKEY SKATES VERSUS FIGURE SKATES

Hockey skate design features	Advantages	Disadvantages
The blade is shorter and is half the width.	It's easier to stop and start quickly. Sharp turns can be performed.	It's less stable.
The blade is more curved and doesn't extend behind the boot.	Faster reactions.	You are even more likely to fall backwards.
No toe-rake on blade – a plain, rounded end instead.	Players stay on the ice – rather than in the air spinning – and toe-rake injuries are avoided.	No stylish jumps of joy when you score a goal!

Hockey skate

Figure skate

The speed skate

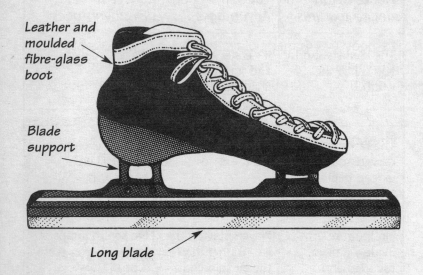

Leather and
moulded
fibre-glass
boot

Blade
support

Long blade

The speed skate blade is longer than the figure skate blade,
thinner, single-edged and straight. The blade can be
unscrewed from the boot within a few minutes.

DID YOU KNOW?
Speed skate blades can be 45cm in length.

The longer blade on the speed skate gives it greater contact with the ice and allows you to glide. Because the blade extends beyond the rear of the boot, you have more stability and are less likely to fall backwards.

The boot itself is made of leather, has a fibre-glass base (or similar) and looks more like a shoe. Unlike the figure skate, it does not support the ankle but allows it to move freely.

ZOOM!

Speed skating is one of the most amazing sports to watch. Wearing lightweight, aerodynamic gear and long skates, top speed skaters can reach speeds of over 45 kilometres per hour – so fast they sometimes fly off the track! It is compulsory for speed skaters to wear hard-shell helmets. Knee- and shin-pads and gloves also provide extra protection from accidents. Turn to page 119 for more information about speed skating.

Should I buy or hire skates?

As a beginner skater it's a good idea to hire these from the rink hire shop until you are sure you want to skate regularly. These skates will be fine for group lessons. Later, if you move on to one-to-one coaching, having your own, well-fitted skates can help your performance. Here are some things to think about when buying skates:

Second hand – but not second best ...

New figure skates can be very expensive, but finding a good-quality pair of second-hand skates could cut your costs in half. Another advantage is that they will have been broken in by someone else!

Second-hand figure skates may be advertised on ice rink notice boards, in skating magazines, club newsletters and some skating shops. Sometimes the hire shop may sell on their skates. **But remember, be wary – a bad fit is scary!** Whatever the quality and good value a second-hand skate seems to offer, if it doesn't fit YOUR foot – forget it!

Top tips for checking used skates

* Don't buy skates that smell nasty – they'll only get worse!
* Avoid boots that have had considerable wear.
* Check inside and outside the boots for holes – you don't want any!
* Make sure all the eyelets for the laces are in place.
* Frayed or worn laces can and must be replaced.
* Make sure the blade is in good order and has not been over-sharpened. See page 40 for more information about this.

TESTING SUPPORT

* Hold the boot by the top of the ankle and turn the skate upside-down so that the blade is at the top.
* Watch to see what happens to the boot: if it falls to either side, it is worn out or poor quality. Forget it! You need a stronger boot than this.
* If a boot has good ankle support, it is very difficult to squeeze its ankle area together when it's off the foot.

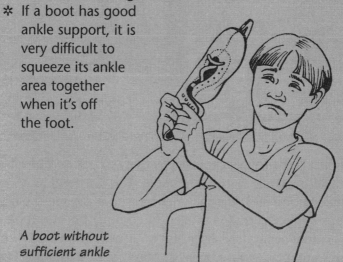

A boot without sufficient ankle support.

New skates

It's best to buy your own skates as soon as possible.

Always buy new skates from a specialist skating shop rather than a general sports shop. You will have more choice, and are also more likely to have the help of an expert fitter.

The first pair of skates you buy is likely to come with a general-purpose figure skate blade. This is a relief as it keeps decisions simple! It is only when you have mastered basic jumps and spins that you need to consider buying boots and blades separately. Prices for your own combination of skates and blades vary between the cost of 6 to 500 CDs! Remember, skates make a great birthday present so start dropping hints now!

Top tips for top skates

✳ Your skate boot should be the same size as your normal shoe size to give you control over your movements. It must be snug enough to support your ankle and foot adequately, but it must also be comfortable.

✳ Leather boots are better than plastic – they last longer and they are more comfortable.

✳ The more layers of leather, the stronger and more supportive (and more expensive) the boot is.

✳ Look for good padding to the heel and ankle for extra comfort.

✳ Make sure the blade is straight and is not bent or warped.

✳ Avoid blades that are riveted to the boot – you need blades that screw to the boot, and can be adjusted.

✳ Are the blades sharp? See page 40 for more advice.

DID YOU KNOW?

Top skaters usually have boots made specially for them – called 'custom-made' boots. They usually wear out at least one pair in a year.

Good-fit figure skates check-list

* Once laced up, a new boot should have about 5cm of space between the lines of the eyelets. This space narrows over time as the boots are worn-in and the leather stretches.

* Your heel should fit securely at the back of the boot and shouldn't move up and down once the boot is laced correctly.

* Toes should be near the end of the boot – touching it lightly, but make sure you can move them and that they're not bent.

* The ball of your foot shouldn't move around inside the boot or rock from side to side.

REMEMBER! At best, badly-fitting boots are uncomfortable. At worst, they can be dangerous!

THE WALK TEST
If the boots seem to fit, leave them on for about 10 minutes and keep walking around in them. If they hurt in places, or seem too loose, try another pair half a size larger or smaller.

Breaking in new skating boots

New boots can be very uncomfortable to begin with. They are stiff and need heat and moisture to soften and mould them to your foot-shape. Here are some suggestions for speeding up the breaking-in process:

✳ Attach blade guards and wear the skates around the house for about 20 minutes. Take your skates off for 15 minutes and put them on again for a further 20 minutes.
✳ Wear a pair of damp socks inside your boots and walk or skate in them for a short while.
✳ If the boots are very stiff, leave the top pair of hooks unlaced and fasten the double-knotted bow below.
✳ Find a good skate shop and ask if they can punch out very sore areas of the boot to ease the pain.

Lacing figure skate boots

1 Loosen the laces, starting at the upper eyelets and
  stopping at the two pairs nearest the toe. Pull the tongue
  upwards and forwards over the front of the skate.
2 Put your foot in the boot, pushing your heel to the very
  back of the boot. Pull up the tongue and tuck in place.
3 Make sure your skate is flat on the floor and your lower
  leg is upright. Then, using both hands, work upwards
  from the toe to pull out the slack from the laces. Pull the
  laces firmly around the ankle.
4 Cross the laces before pulling them around the hooks –
  one pair at a time. Make sure you don't pull the laces too
  tightly around the final pair of hooks.

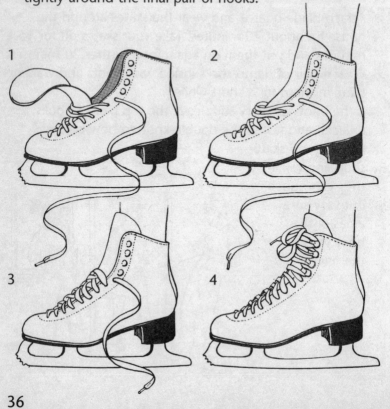

Top tips for tip-top lacing

✳ Before tying the laces in a double-knotted bow at the top, make sure you can bend your knees while standing. If you can't, the lacing is too tight around your ankle.

✳ To prevent the laces and their loops getting caught around the hooks of the opposite boot, tuck them down between the tongue and the laces. Very short loops can be attached to the hooks below.

✳ To avoid accidents never wrap long laces around the top of your skate. Get shorter laces instead and remember to tuck any loose ends into your boot.

REMEMBER! Boots need to be firmly laced for control, but not too tight for comfort!

What about blades?

Where should they be fitted?

For most people, blades should be fitted centrally on the boot's sole – running from beneath the centre of your heel to the space between your big toe and its neighbour.

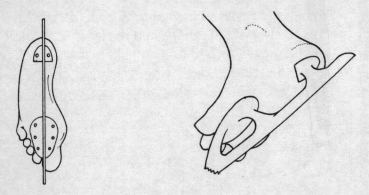

Once correctly positioned, your blades should allow you to glide in a straight line along the ice as you skate forwards. If you find your blades pull either to the left or right they probably need re-positioning. An experienced coach or the skate shop should be able to advise you.

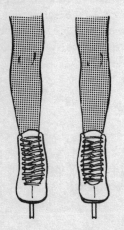

These blades are correctly fitted allowing the skater to stand upright with ease. With weight evenly over both the inside and outside edges, skating in a straight line should (with practice) be easy!

Problem positioning

If you and your skates can't agree on where you are going
life can be frustrating ...

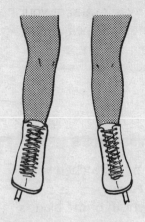

*These blades are positioned too
far to the outside causing the
feet to lean inwards. With the
skater's weight forced onto the
inside edges, the skates move
outwards.* **Remedy:** *move the
blades inwards.*

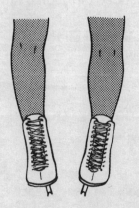

*These blades are positioned too
far to the inside causing the feet
to lean outwards. The skater's
weight is forced onto the outside
edges making the skates move
inwards.* **Remedy:** *move the
blades outwards.*

INTERMEDIATE SKATERS: TESTING TIP FOR FINE TUNING

Try transferring your weight from the outside edge to the inside edge while skating forwards. A badly positioned blade will pull you the wrong way. Have your blades repositioned as explained on page 39.

Sharp skates

A figure skate blade needs sharpening when ...

✳ The surface of your fingernail is not scratched when rubbed across the width of the edges.

✳ Running your finger along the length of the blade's underside, the two edges feel rounded or rough – rather than sharp and clean.

✳ While skating you find it difficult to push off the ice without your edges slipping sideways.

FIGURE SKATE SHARPENING – DOs AND DON'TS

✳ Do ask your coach to recommend a sharpener – quality of work can vary.

✳ Do use a figure skate sharpener – a hockey skate sharpener may not have the necessary experience or equipment.

✳ Do be prepared to pay a little more for sharpening figure skate blades than for hockey skate blades.

✳ Don't allow a sharpener to shave off the bottom of your toe-rake – no matter how many times you trip over it!

Looking after skates

❋ Use a special skate wax to waterproof the soles of your boots.

❋ Clean and polish the outsides of your boots regularly and use a colour restorer from time to time to revive them.

❋ Have your blades sharpened regularly.

❋ Save yourself embarrassment by checking the screws in the base of your blades before you skate – they may need tightening.

❋ Whenever you are wearing your skates off ice, put skate guards on the blades. These are made from plastic or rubber and will protect your edges from being worn down, scratched or damaged.

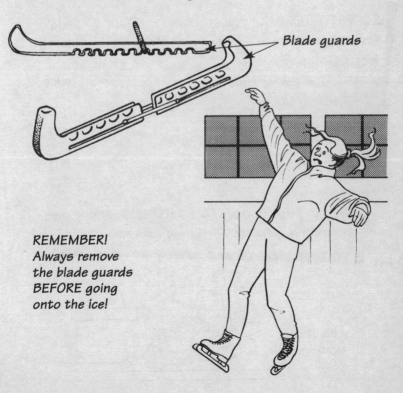

Blade guards

REMEMBER!
Always remove
the blade guards
BEFORE going
onto the ice!

Rest not rust

Although blades are made from chrome-plated stainless steel, they can rust easily if not kept dry. *Always:*

❋ Remove blade guards when storing your skates as any moisture inside the guards may cause rust patches to form.

❋ Wipe your skates with a towelling cloth as soon as you come off the ice.

❋ Clean and polish your blades regularly.

❋ Store skates in a dry place.

❋ Use absorbent skate-guards when your blades are not in use.

ACCESSORIES KIT

Keep these and you'll keep your skates looking great!

✳ Blade guards
✳ Absorbent skate-guards
✳ Towelling cloth
✳ Blade polish
✳ Boot polish and colour restorer
✳ Polishing cloths
✳ Screwdriver
✳ Spare laces
✳ Washing-up sponge (1cm thickness), 'animal wool' or 'bubble wrap' for extra comfort in boots

*Absorbent
skate-guards*

4 Skating basics

**warming up • posture • balance •
falling safely • edges**

Avoid the rush!

Allow yourself plenty of time before your skating lesson.
The exact amount of time this will take can vary
depending on how busy the rink is. Here's a rough guide:

- 5 minutes: Queuing for your ticket and finding your
  skating coach.
- 15 minutes: Being fitted with suitable hire skates
  (if you've skated before).
- 30 minutes: Being fitted with suitable hire skates
  (if it's your first time).
- 15 minutes: Warming up your muscles for the cold
  conditions of the ice rink – essential!
- 10 minutes: Practice time
  for wearing your boots
  off the ice (if you are
  a first-time skater).

If you are a first-time skater,
it could be between 35
minutes and an hour before
you set foot on the ice!
Make sure you don't rush
the skate-fitting or skip on
the off-ice practice and
warm-up.

Warming up for the ice

As with all sports, it is important to warm up before ice skating and to keep warm. Ice rinks can be very cool places, making muscle injury more likely if your body isn't prepared. If you try to work all your main muscles with a few simple exercises you will: improve your flexibility; help your balance; protect your muscles and raise your heart rate.

After you come off the ice you will need to do some further stretching exercises to cool down and relax your muscles. Ask your coach to show you the exercises that he or she recommends you do before and after skating. It's important for you to learn them correctly – and to always do them!

Off-ice practice

Before you step onto the rink, take advantage of the non-slippery, rubber floor-surface around the rink as a practice area. Put on your skate guards and try the following:

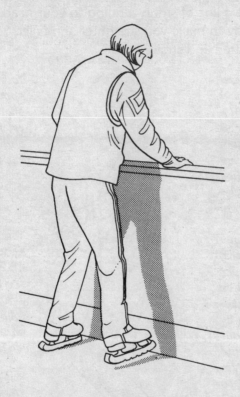

❋ Hold onto the boards that surround the rink and practise standing and transferring your weight from one foot to the other. This is great for practising your balance.

❋ Now try the same without holding onto the boarding.

❋ Practise walking around the area.

Next we need to think about posture and how to hold yourself on the ice ...

Head, shoulders, knees and ... posture!

Good posture is a priority if you are to look elegant on the ice. Imagine a line of string running to your head, pulling up your body to make you straighter and taller. Your neck should be lifted and straight.

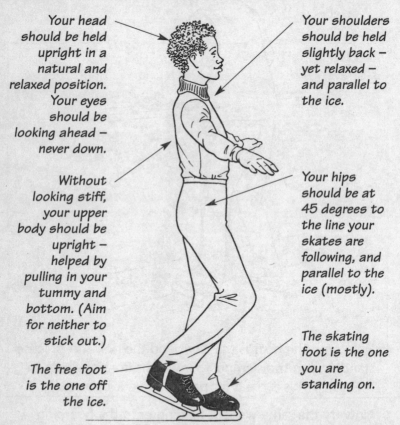

Your head should be held upright in a natural and relaxed position. Your eyes should be looking ahead – never down.

Your shoulders should be held slightly back – yet relaxed – and parallel to the ice.

Without looking stiff, your upper body should be upright – helped by pulling in your tummy and bottom. (Aim for neither to stick out.)

Your hips should be at 45 degrees to the line your skates are following, and parallel to the ice (mostly).

The free foot is the one off the ice.

The skating foot is the one you are standing on.

Your skating leg should be bent at the knee and should be constantly bending up and down to assist your moves. Never fully stretch your skating knee or bend it to its limit when skating as this may bring your movements to a sudden stop.

REMEMBER!

❊ Shoulders should be relaxed – not raised.

❊ Arms should extend gracefully in a slight curve.

❊ Hands should be held at waist height, with palms held naturally and facing the ice.

❊ Fingers should be neither clenched nor extended, but relaxed.

POSTURE POINTERS

Wherever you see this pair of skaters in the book, look at their elegant posture and position and remind yourself to do the same.

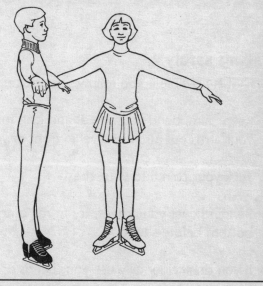

Skating aim

When you start skating, aim to make it look as effortless, graceful and flowing as possible. This is achieved through good posture, mastering techniques and lots of practice.

Make it a good fall!

Don't worry about falling. Everyone, from beginners to top skaters, takes a tumble from time to time. In fact, learning to fall and repeatedly practising it (whether you mean to or not!) is the first lesson of skating. To prevent injuries, however, learn to fall safely. If you do it well, you'll just slide along the ice!

Top tip for topples

Always try to fall forwards to protect the back of your head and try not to use your hands to break your fall.

Falling safely

Yes – it is possible if you follow this advice!

1 Keep calm, bend your knees and lean forwards. Hold your arms out at chest-level in front of you.

2 Tuck your chin into your chest.

3 Bending over your knees, try to roll onto one side of your bottom before sitting.

4 If you do accidentally use your hands or arms, draw them quickly to your body for protection from other skaters.

5 When you land on the ice, allow your body to glide across it as this will absorb much of the force.

YOU KNOW YOU'RE GAINING CONFIDENCE WHEN ...
You fall over! It shows you're being adventurous and trying to improve.

Skating ups and downs ...

❋ After a fall, try to get up swiftly to avoid getting too cold and wet. Try not to lie down like an injured footballer on ice – not everyone on the rink is looking where they are going!

❋ To get up, put your hands flat onto the ice and lean forwards onto your knees.

❋ Lift your right knee in front of you and position your right skate blade into an upright position on the ice. With both hands to your sides, push yourself up while placing your left foot into position alongside. Try to put equal weight on both feet.

Getting up after a fall

49

Getting the edge

If you truly understand how your blades work you'll get on a lot better on the ice! First, look at the narrow base. You will see the hollow along its length with an edge on either side: you'll remember that one is the inside edge; the other is the outside edge. All your movements from pushing off and skating curves and circles, to creating spins and jumps will depend on the control of these edges.

On the edge(s)

Practise finding your edges like this:

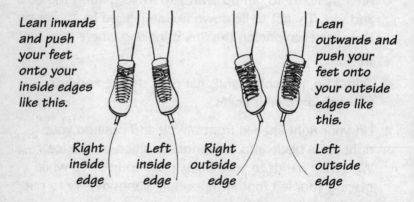

Lean inwards and push your feet onto your inside edges like this.

Lean outwards and push your feet onto your outside edges like this.

Right inside edge

Left inside edge

Right outside edge

Left outside edge

SKATING ON DEEP EDGES

The closer the blade of the skating foot leans towards the ice, the deeper the edge. When skaters use deep edges they are more able to grip the ice well. This makes sharp curves and some amazing angles of skating possible. Deep edges demand great control and skill and they're perfect for impressing the competition judges!

Backwards and forwards ...

The blade is slightly curved along its length – this is called the radius (or rocker). This curve allows you to move your weight from the front to the back of the blade. Your weight needs to be on the back section of the blade when skating forwards, and slightly closer to the centre when skating backwards.

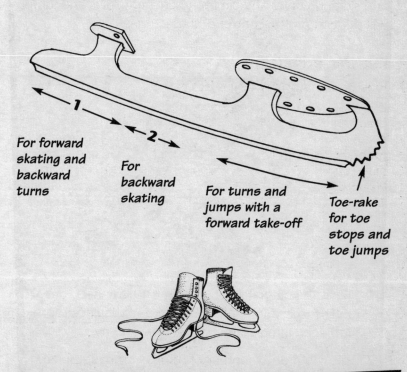

1 For forward skating and backward turns

2 For backward skating

For turns and jumps with a forward take-off

Toe-rake for toe stops and toe jumps

MOST USED EDGE
Most beginners find it more natural to stand on their inside edges. But remember to practise standing on the outside edges as these are really the ones you will need the most.

QUICK QUIZ – TEST YOUR INSTINCTS!

What should you do if you lose your balance?

1 Aim to stay tall and upright to miss the ice, while throwing your arms upwards.
2 Grab onto the nearest person.
3 Bend and crouch down to touch your knees or toes.

Answers

1 This is the natural reaction of most beginners, but rarely successful. It lifts your centre of balance too high, increasing your chances of falling over.

2. This could do a number of things – from stopping your fall to landing on a total stranger! It's not recommended – though an interesting way to meet people ...

3. Your best bet for regaining balance – a tactic that works nearly every time as it brings your centre of balance closer to the ice.

5 Let's go skating forwards!

stopping • dips • sculling • gliding • stroking

Here goes ... breaking the ice!

Have no fear if you're stepping on the ice for the first time. Here are some tips to help you.

1 Make sure you remove your blade guards and put them in your bag or locker before stepping on the ice. Hold onto the boards (barrier) to steady yourself while removing the guards.

2 On the ice, turn to face the boards and hold on with both hands. Place your skates in a 'V'-position and practise bending your knees up and down so that your shins touch the top of the tongues in your skates.

3 In the same position, practise lifting one foot at a time as you bend your knees. When you feel confident, let go of the boards!

First steps!

Pointing your toes outwards gives your edges a surface to push against, making movements forwards more effective.

1 In the start position, stand up tall and place your feet in the 'V'-position with your heels together and toes facing outwards.

2 Bending your knees, lift your right skate off the ice by about 5cm.

3 Place your right skate on the ice slightly in front of your left skate at almost 90 degrees outwards.

4 Repeat this move with your left skate.

5 Keep going and see if you can begin to glide a little on your skating foot – the leading foot on the ice.

1   2   3   4   5

Forward sculling

If skating on the ice one foot at a time makes you feel a little wobbly, try sculling – then both feet stay on the ice!

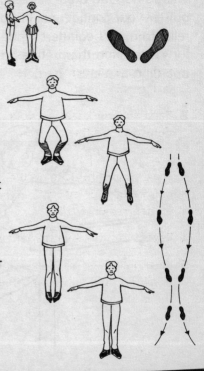

1 In the start position, stand up tall in the 'V'-position as before.

2 Bend your knees deeply and press your weight evenly onto your inside edges to move forwards.

3 Keep your knees bent and let your feet glide forwards and outwards until they are about 50cm apart.

4 Straighten your knees when your skates are parallel, push your heels outwards and your toes inwards to bring your feet together. This is one complete movement.

5 When your feet are parallel repeat from step 2.

HELP!

Q. My feet won't glide apart easily!

A. Ease your knees! The more you bend them, the easier it is to use your inside edges: the more you use your inside edges, the further apart your feet will glide.

Q. I can't travel in a straight line!

A. Try to keep your feet parallel and your weight evenly over your feet. Check your hips are facing forwards and that they are parallel to the ice.

Confidence booster – Learning to stop!

There's nothing quite like learning to stop properly to bolster your confidence. It looks impressive and comes as a relief to most beginners who – thrilled to be skating forwards – find themselves bruised from using the rink boarding as a crash barrier!

There are three basic methods of stopping on skates:

1 The snowplough stop – the easiest.
2 The T-stop – a simple stop that looks elegant.
3 The hockey stop – the most advanced stop, and the one that produces a spray of ice when performed with speed!

Most beginners start with the snowplough. It is an effective means of stopping but takes some practice to get it right. The aim is to place your feet in an upside-down 'V'-shape (the snowplough) before sliding a few metres to a stop. See how you get on!

The snowplough stop

1 You'll need to gather speed first so, standing tall with your arms out to the sides, start skating forwards in a straight line.
Continue until you have gained some speed.

2 To stop, place your feet about 50 cm apart and bend your knees strongly. Make sure your arms are perfectly still and outstretched.

3 Bending your knees further, turn your toes inwards to make the snowplough, while pushing your skates forwards and outwards.

4 Press gently onto your inside edges, push your heels outwards and hold your position as you slide.

5 Concentrate on sliding in a straight line until you stop.

Keep your eyes looking forwards at all times.

Keep your hips and shoulders parallel to the ice.

WHOOPS!
Never let your toes or knees touch while doing a snowplough stop!

Once you get the hang of the snowplough stop, try skating a little faster into the stop and holding the position for at least three seconds.

The T-stop

1 Again, gather speed as before. When you're ready to stop, glide on one foot, bend the knee of your leading leg and put your weight onto that foot – your skating foot.

2 Meanwhile, lift your free foot and place it behind and at a right angle to your skating foot. Your free foot should hover above the ice.

3 Making sure your arms are perfectly still and outstretched, place your free foot gently down on the ice. Tilt your free foot towards its inside edge and drag it behind your skating foot until you stop.

The hockey stop

All the practice this impressive stop requires is worth it!

1 Gather speed as before. When you are ready to stop, stretch your arms out to your sides while keeping your shoulders at right angles to the direction of your skates.

2 Keeping your upper body still and your feet together, bend your knees and quickly rotate your hips and skates to either the left or the right – whichever is most comfortable. Straighten your knees a little.

3 With your weight evenly over both feet, bend your knees sharply to skid to a stop.

One foot at a time

Here you begin to learn the basics of forward stroking – the elegant way experienced skaters cross the ice (see pages 65-66). Try to practise this as much as possible.

1 In the start position, stand up tall and place your right foot at 90 degrees in front of your left foot.

FROM RIGHT FOOT AS SKATING FOOT ...

2 Bend your knees, gently push your front (right) skate forwards and transfer your weight onto the outside edge. This is now your skating foot. Extend your left leg (free leg) behind.

3 Bring your left foot back to its original position, next to the leading foot.

... TO LEFT FOOT AS SKATING FOOT

4 Bend your knees and gently push your left foot forwards on its outside edge. Transfer your weight onto this – your skating foot – and place your right foot behind it, and extend your leg.

5 Keep repeating these actions and see how far you go!

CUTTING EDGE
* Always hold your arms out to the side with your hands face downwards at hip level.
* Try not to lean forwards with your upper body.

The glide and dip

This is a great exercise for practising your balance and control while bending down towards the ice.

1 In the start position, stand up tall and place your right foot at 90 degrees in front of your left foot.

NOW PREPARE TO GLIDE ...

2 Push your right foot forwards and transfer your body weight onto the outside edge.

3 Bring your rear (left) foot back to its position next to the leading (right) foot and then push the left foot forwards. Make a number of forward pushes on one foot and then the next.

4 Place your feet side by side and glide.

THEN DIP ...

5 Slowly bend your knees and hold out your arms in front of you.

6 Lower your hips until they are just lower than your knees. Hold the position.

CUTTING EDGE
Make sure your shoulders are parallel to the ice. As you glide your arms should be out to the sides and slightly forwards.

Tips for dips!

To keep your balance and prevent a backward tumble, concentrate on pushing your weight forwards through your arms as you bend into the dip.

The dip challenge

See how low you can dip your hips without losing your balance. Can you:

1 Continue to bend your knees so that your bottom is just 10cm or so off the ice?

2 Touch your toes, straighten your knees and return to standing?

CUTTING EDGE

✳ To stand you will need to straighten your knees gradually while keeping your weight on the heels of your feet. Place your arms forwards for balance.

Dips for sits!

If you need to practise falling and getting up, the dip is the best starting point for the fall. Simply find a dry area of ice, bend your knees as above and sit down!
Turn to pages 48-49 if you've forgotten the rest!

Forward glide on one foot

Here you have the one-foot-at-a-time forward movement (see page 59), with the addition of a gliding movement and an extended free leg. Once you've mastered this, you'll be on your way to the forward stroking method (pages 65-66) used by all good skaters.

RIGHT FOOT AS SKATING FOOT

1 Stand up tall with your right arm and the right side of your body angled slightly forwards and your left arm to the side. Look ahead.

2 Place your feet together at 90 degrees with your right foot forwards.

3 Bend both your knees and gently push onto the outside edge of your right (front) skate while transferring your weight onto that foot (your skating foot). Keep your skating leg bent. At the same time, lift and stretch your left leg (free leg) behind, turning your foot to its side and pointing your toes.
As you raise your free leg, you will be gliding forwards on a slight outward curve. Well done!

62

LEFT FOOT AS SKATING FOOT

4 Bring your feet together at 90 degrees with your left foot forwards and your legs straight. Bring your left arm and left side of your body slightly forwards while your right arm is to the side.

5 Bend both your knees and gently push onto the outside edge of your leading (left) skate and transfer your weight to that foot (now your skating foot), keeping your skating leg bent. Glide forwards on your skating foot in an outward curve, while lifting and extending your free leg behind as before. Bring your feet together and repeat from 2.

CUTTING EDGE

✳ Remember to avoid lunging forward with each movement.

Extended forward glide

This is a progression from the forward glide on one foot on the previous pages. It increases the time you spend gliding on the skating foot. It does take some practice but you'll look impressive!

RIGHT FOOT AS SKATING FOOT

1 Repeat steps 1 to 5 for the forward glide on one foot. As you are gliding on your skating foot (right), lower your free leg and place your foot 5cm off the ice alongside your skating foot. Hold your free foot in contact with the skating foot before placing it on the ice alongside.

2 Repeat this move with your left foot as the skating foot.

Hold your free foot 5cm off the ice – in contact with your skating foot – and glide.

CUTTING EDGE

✳ Make sure your extended free leg is held in line behind your skating leg.

✳ To help you to tilt your right skate onto its outside edge, make sure your body weight is slightly to the right. Vice versa for your left skate.

Forward stroking

You've made it! Here we have the ultimate forward skating move – a pushing movement. Stroking uses the inside edge of your non-skating foot as a base for your gliding foot to push off from.

1 In the start position, stand up tall with your heels together.

RIGHT FOOT AS SKATING FOOT

2 Bend both your knees and place your feet together at 90 degrees with your right foot forwards.

3 Use the inside edge of your left foot (your pushing foot) to push against the ice. Glide forwards on the outside edge of your right foot (your skating foot), lift your left foot off the ice and extend the free leg (left) behind your skating leg and point your toes. Hold the glide for 2 seconds or more.

4 Bring your feet back slowly together and straighten your legs a little.

Let's go skating forwards!

LEFT FOOT AS SKATING FOOT

5 Bend your knees and place your feet together at 90 degrees with your left foot forwards.

6 Transfer your weight to the inside edge of your right foot – your 'new' pushing foot – push onto the outside edge of your left foot and glide. At the same time gracefully raise and extend your right leg behind you and point your toes. Glide for 2 seconds or more and bring your feet slowly back together.

Repeat steps 2 to 6 to continue. You did it!

CUTTING EDGE
* Keep your hips and shoulders facing forwards.
* Make sure your knees are bent to make a stronger push.
* Avoid lunging with each movement – try to keep your upper body still.

Forward stroking challenge

Practise stroking as much as possible. Aim to do seven or more similar strokes one after the other.

Forward to backward two-foot turn

By now you're getting to grips with skating forwards, and you'll be learning how to skate backwards in the next chapter. This is the turn you will see beginner skaters use to turn from forwards to backwards.

1 To start, stand up tall, place your feet together at 90 degrees with your right foot leading, bend your knees and glide or skate forwards.

TURNING TO THE RIGHT

2 Place your feet side by side and turn your upper body to face right. Rotate your left arm and shoulder in front and your right arm and shoulder behind. Meanwhile, both hands should be at hip level with palms facing down, and you should continue to look in the direction you are moving.

3 Bend your knees and – using a powerful movement – quickly turn both feet and hips (shoulders remain still) 180 degrees clockwise, straightening your knees during the turn and bending them again afterwards.

4 Keep your arms and shoulders facing right and allow yourself to glide backwards while looking in the direction you are travelling.

Let's go skating forwards!

TURNING TO THE LEFT
Follow steps to 4 but for every 'right' read it as 'left'. So, with your right arm and shoulder in front and your left arm and shoulder behind, your upper body will be facing left before turning 180 degrees anti-clockwise.

CUTTING EDGE

✳ As you turn, your weight should be transferred to the balls of your feet. It should return to the middle of the blades for your glide.
✳ Keep your momentum going during the turn by:
  ● Keeping your toe-rake off the ice.
  ● Rotating your feet and hips as quickly as possible for the turn.

Exercise, exercise, exercise ... regularly!

To progress quickly with your skating, you will need to build up strength and flexibility. Weight training is great for developing strength, while stretching exercises will improve your flexibility. Aerobic exercise such as cycling or swimming – when performed regularly – will increase your stamina for all those laps of the rink!

Let's go skating backwards!

gliding • sculling • snowplough • stroking

Time for a change of scene!

Skating backwards gives you a new outlook on life! Always remember to look behind you to make sure the rink is clear before setting off.

Backward sculling

This is simply a reverse of the forward sculling movement you learnt earlier.

The starting position for skating backwards.

1 To start, stand up tall, turn your toes inwards, your heels outwards and place your weight evenly over the balls of your feet. You will be standing towards the front of your blades, but make sure you're not on the toe-rakes!

2 Bend your knees, press onto your inside edges and let your feet glide apart. Make sure your skates move at the same time and the same speed.

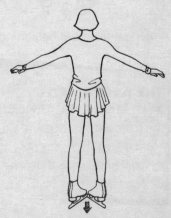

69

3 When your skates are about 50cm apart and parallel, straighten your knees and turn your heels inwards. Let your feet glide in a parallel position before bringing them together with your toes facing outwards. This is one sculling movement.

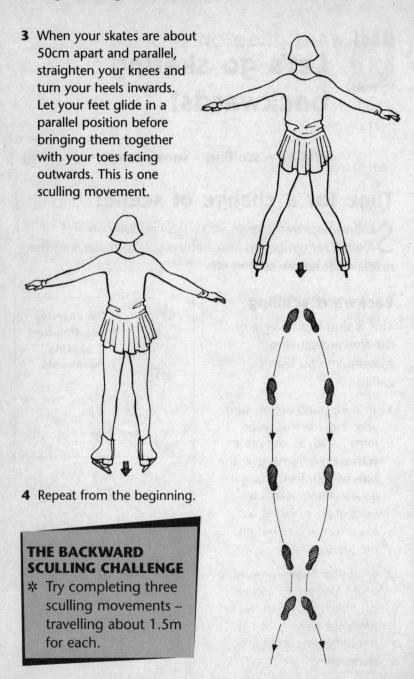

4 Repeat from the beginning.

THE BACKWARD SCULLING CHALLENGE

✳ Try completing three sculling movements – travelling about 1.5m for each.

Backward glide on two feet

Here you can make use of the backward sculling movement to start you off in a gliding motion. This is a gentle introduction to the backward glide on one foot on the next page.

CUTTING EDGE

✻ To glide smoothly you will need to have your weight on the balls of your feet. It's important, however, not to lean so far forwards that your toe-rakes slow your movement.

1 Get into the same starting position as before:

2 Follow steps 1 to 4 on pages 69-70 and begin sculling backwards to gain some momentum.

3 Once you have gained some speed, leave your feet in the parallel position when they are back together and allow yourself to glide backwards.

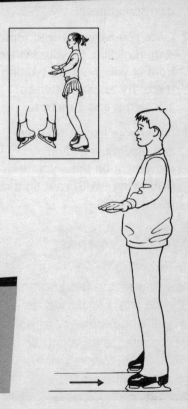

THE TWO-FOOT BACKWARD GLIDE CHALLENGE

✻ Try to glide for between 1.5 and 2 metres!

Backward glide on one foot

As you guessed, the reverse of gliding forwards!

CUTTING EDGE

* Your hips and shoulders must be parallel and facing directly forwards to glide in a straight line.

* Remember to check that no one is behind you before you start!

1 To start, stand up tall and following steps 1-3 on pages 69-70, begin sculling backwards to gain some speed.

2 Once you have gathered some speed and have started gliding, lift your left leg (free leg) in front of your right leg (skating leg) and hold it there. Try to glide between 1.5 metres and 2 metres.

3 Lower your left leg (free leg) and repeat the gliding movement on this – your new skating leg – with your right leg raised in front.

Wobble worries!

If wobbling over is your worry, practise holding onto the boards and letting go as you lift one foot. Try to hold your balance for a couple of seconds before reaching out for the boards.

72

Backward snowplough

You've already learnt the forward snowplough so this should be easy! It's the same idea except that, with your feet slightly further apart, you point your toes outwards rather than inwards.

CUTTING EDGE
* ❋ When you're ready to stop, place your hands above your knees and lean forwards slightly.

1 Standing up tall and following steps 1 to 3 on page 72, look behind you and begin gliding backwards on one foot at a time to gather some speed.

2 When you are ready to stop, make sure your feet are slightly apart and parallel.

3 Bend your knees, press onto your inside edges and push your feet apart. Your toes should be pointing outwards as you bring yourself to a stop.

WAS IT A GOOD STOP?
* ❋ If you managed to scrape a layer off the ice surface, you're doing well!

Backward stroking

Your backward skating technique will look even more professional once you have mastered this move.

1 Begin by standing up tall in the start position, with your toes pointed inwards, your heels outwards and your arms extended to the sides.

2 Bend your knees, keep your left skate on the ice and transfer your weight to your right foot. Push off with the inside edge of your right foot and transfer your weight to your left foot. Move your left hip back slightly at the same time.

3 Bend your left leg (skating leg) and extend your right leg (free leg) in front of you, turning out your foot. At the same time, move your free arm (right) forwards and your skating arm (left) slightly back.

4 Hold this position for a few seconds, and place your free foot alongside your skating foot while straightening your skating leg (to a relaxed position).

5 Repeat steps 2 to 4 with your left foot (read 'right' for 'left' and vice versa).

Backward to forward turn

For this move you will be skating backwards on one foot, turning 180 degrees and then stepping forwards on the opposite foot.

1 Start by standing up tall with your toes inwards. Hold your arms out to the side and bend your knees. Glide backwards onto your right foot (your skating foot), and lift your left foot (your free foot) in front. Bring your feet together and glide on your left foot (your skating foot) and then your right.

2 With your left foot (your free foot) in front, move your left shoulder back, and turn your head to the left.

3 Place your heels together and your toes outwards and step forwards on the outside edge of your left foot. With a strong movement, pull back your right shoulder at the same time to help you turn in a clockwise direction.

4 Stay on the forward outside edge as you turn.

5 If you prefer to turn with your right foot, follow the instructions for 1 to 4, but read 'right' for 'left' and 'anti-clockwise' for 'clockwise' each time.

7 Moving on

**crossovers • three-turns •
the outside edges • mohawk**

Private coaching

By this stage you may find it helpful to have a private coaching session to work on your technique. If this is too expensive, try to team up with a friend or two for a semi-private lesson. This way you can share the cost between you and still have plenty of expert attention.

A record of your progress ...

How about making a 'skating diary'? Use it to write down one or two realistic goals before each skating session. After the session, record the moves you practised, how close you came to your goals and any special tips that you learnt. Make a note of anything that you need to work on. The diary should help you to really focus on your skating as well as becoming a record of your progress.

Practice makes perfect!

Try to stay for half an hour after each lesson. Run through the lesson again and work on the moves you found difficult. If you can afford one or two extra practice sessions between coaching sessions you will progress even faster.

Spotlight

World ice dance stars, Jayne Torvill and Christopher Dean (UK) recognise the importance of practice. They think nothing of repeating the same move up to 1000 times!

In 1984 at the World Ice Dance Championships in Ottawa, Canada, Torvill and Dean's dedication to perfection paid off. They broke all records in being awarded 29 perfect marks. This was the highest number ever scored at a single international championship – a world record for ice dance perfection – and a figure that brought their amateur career total for 6.0s (the highest possible score) to 136. There were yet more to follow in 1994!

Judges considered their presentations so outstanding that on four occasions they were awarded perfect sets of figures (nine 6.0s):

***1983** World Championships at Helsinki, Finland*
   Nine 6.0s – presentation in the free dance

***1984** Winter Olympics at Sarajevo, Yugoslavia*
   Nine 6.0s – presentation in the free dance competition

***1984** World Championships at Ottawa, Canada*
   Nine 6.0s – presentation in the set pattern dance
   Nine 6.0s – presentation in free dance

1	2	3	4	5	6	7	8	9
6.0	6.0	6.0	6.0	6.0	6.0	6.0	6.0	6.0

Forward crossovers

Crossovers enable you to skate around corners or to follow a curve. One crossover is made up of two steps (the first on an outside edge; the second on an inside edge) and two pushes.

Aim: to skate forwards in a circle in an anti-clockwise or clockwise direction, while holding your free arm forwards and your skating arm behind.

1 To move anti-clockwise start by standing tall, place your feet together at 90 degrees with your left skate leading.

2 With your right arm (free arm) leading, bend your knees, push off onto the outside edge of your left skate and glide on a curve with your skating leg (left) bent. At the same time, extend your free leg (right) and turn out the free foot.

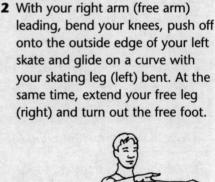

3 Balancing on the outside edge of your skating foot, carefully bring your free leg forwards.

4 Leaning into the curve, and keeping your right arm forwards, cross your right leg over your skating leg.

5 Transfer your weight to the inside edge of your right skate. Meanwhile begin to extend your left leg (free leg) backwards.

6 Carefully bring your feet together into the starting position with your left foot leading.

7 Repeat steps 2 to 6.

8 Now try skating forward crossovers in a clockwise direction.

CUTTING EDGE

✻ Make sure your pushes are from the edge of the blade and not from the toe-rake!

✻ Keep your skating knee bent at all times: this gives you a powerful pushing movement and prevents you from catching your toe-rake.

✻ Try to keep your shoulders, arms and hips in the same position throughout and remember to keep your back straight.

✻ Avoid holding your crossing foot out to the side before crossing it over your skating foot.

✻ Try not to glide for too long on two feet between crossovers.

✻ Practise in both clockwise and anti-clockwise directions. (Gliding on two feet should be avoided.)

Backward crossovers

If you have ever seen top skaters performing amazing jumps, you will have seen them perform backward crossovers beforehand to gather speed.

Aim: to skate backwards in a circle in a clockwise or anti-clockwise direction, while holding your right arm forwards and your left arm behind.

1 To move clockwise, start by standing tall with your toes together and your weight on your inside edges. Hold your right arm outstretched in front, your left arm behind and face into the 'circle' you are about to skate.

2 Looking in the direction of your left hand – but not at it – bend your knees strongly and push off backwards onto the outside edge of your left skate and glide in a curve. Raise your free leg (right) in front, point your toes and turn your upper body slightly to the left.

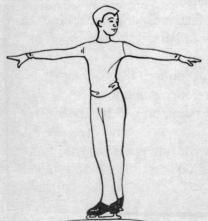

3 Leaning into the 'circle', carefully cross your free leg (right) over your skating leg (left).

4 Transfer your weight to the inside edge of your right skate, bend your new skating leg sharply and begin to extend your left leg (free leg) behind you. Meanwhile keep your eyes focused on the direction in which you are travelling, while keeping your left hand in sight – but not looking directly at it!

5 Carefully bring your feet together into the starting position. Congratulations ... you have completed one backward crossover!

6 Repeat steps 2 to 4.

7 Now try anti-clockwise backward crossovers. Read 'right' for 'left' and vice versa.

CUTTING EDGE
* Remember to look where you are going!
* To help you balance keep your arms outstetched and hands at waist height.
* Lean your upper body slightly towards the centre of the circle.
* Keep your skating leg bent.

The three-turn (forward outside to inside)

You'll find this turn useful – it's one of the turns most frequently seen in ice skating. It's also a key move in ice dancing.

Once you have learnt the three-turn you will be able to:

✳ Turn from forwards to backwards or vice versa.
✳ Change from one edge to the other on the same foot while turning from forwards to backwards.
✳ Rotate in the same direction as the curve you are skating.

CUTTING EDGE
✳ Keep your eyes focused on something ahead of you – as you start to skate – and keep focused on this as you turn and finish.

Aim: To turn from forwards to backwards in an anti-clockwise direction.

1 Start by standing up tall with your heels together, hands at waist height with your right arm leading.

2 Bend your knees and push off onto the outside edge of your right skate. Lift and extend your free leg (left) behind you and turn out the foot. Meanwhile turn your whole body slightly so that the right side is slightly further forwards.

3 Before the turn, bring your straightened left arm and shoulder forwards and take your right arm and shoulder behind at the same time – the reverse of before.

4 Lower your free leg (left) and bring the foot to form a 'T'-shape behind your right foot.

5 Keeping your feet in the 'T'-position, turn your hips and waist strongly to the left to turn from forwards to backwards. Keep your body facing into the circle. When you have turned 180 degrees, straighten your right knee and you will be on the inside edge of your right skate and moving in a backward direction. Your free leg should still be in the 'T'-position behind.

6 Bring your feet together after the turn and change their positions so that your left foot becomes your skating foot (on the outside edge gliding backwards).

To perform the three-turn in a clockwise direction, read 'left' for 'right' and 'right' for 'left' in the instructions.

three-turn
(forward inside to outside)

Aim: to turn in an anti-clockwise direction, starting on a forward inside edge and finishing on a backward outside edge after tracing a number 3 on the ice.

1 Start by standing with your feet together at 90 degrees, with your right foot leading. Hold your left arm and shoulder out in front of you and your right arm slightly behind.

2 Bend your knees and glide onto the inside edge of your right foot while extending your free leg behind you.

3 Lower your free leg and bring your feet together in a 'T'-shape with your right foot leading. Bring your right arm and shoulder forwards.

4 Take your left arm and shoulder backwards slightly – the reverse of before. With your feet in the 'T'-position, quickly turn your waist and hips around to the left while straightening your right knee. Remember to keep your body facing into the 'circle'.

5 After turning 180 degrees to the left, transfer your weight to the outside edge of your left foot and glide backwards.

Warming up on ice

As well as your 'off-ice' warm-up, you should develop a skating warm-up routine. Start with forward and backward stroking and crossovers to get your body moving and gradually add more difficult moves.

CUTTING EDGE

When you watch experienced skaters, their movements look graceful and light. Here are a few tips:

* Maintain a soft rise and fall of the skating leg.
* Try to create a flowing movement while skating by trying to keep your skates following the line of the previous edges.
* Except for such moves as the spread eagle, you should rarely have your weight on both skates at the same time when skating.

Eye, eye, eye!

As you become a more experienced skater, your eyes will look over whichever shoulder is leading. You won't need to look directly at your leading hand, but it should be in view.

Forward outside edges

Skating only on the outside edge may take some practice, but creating perfect circles can be a great challenge!

1 To move in a clockwise direction, start with your heels together and your right foot forwards, extend your right arm forwards and hold your left arm and left side slightly back.

2 Bend your knees sharply. Pushing off from the inside edge of your left skate, transfer your weight to your right skate and glide onto the outside edge. Lean towards the 'circle' while extending your free leg (left) behind you and turning out your foot.

3 Turn your body slightly to the left and let your skating side lead you round the curve.

4 Straightening your skating leg, lower your free foot (left) and hold it briefly in front of your skating foot (right).

5 Bend your skating leg slightly and bring your free leg forwards, extending it in front of you.

6 Lower your arms and, turning on the curve, bring your left arm forwards and move your right arm backwards slightly. Move your weight towards the new 'circle' while bringing your free leg slightly across your skating leg. You are now ready to skate a new 'circle'.

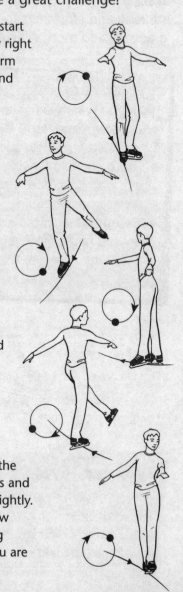

Backward outside edges

Backward outside edges is a great test of control as you try to skate on a circle. The more control you have, the better the circle!

1 To move in an anti-clockwise direction, start by standing up tall with your left arm leading and your right arm held slightly behind you. Face into the 'circle' and bend your knees.

2 Glide backwards in an anti-clockwise direction onto the outside edge of your right foot. Meanwhile, raise your free foot (left) and hold it directly in front of your skating foot (right).

3 Hold your skating side (right) back slightly and look in the direction in which you are travelling.

4 Hold your position until you have completed a semi-circle.

5 Lower your free foot (left) and begin to rotate your upper body and arms to the left.

6 As your skate touches the ice, you should be facing and leaning towards the outside edge of the 'circle'.

7 Trying not to wobble, raise your free leg behind you to finish.

Forward outside open mohawk

Here we have an important method of turning from forwards to backwards that you will see in ice hockey, free skating and ice dancing. The turn is made from forwards to backwards by changing from one foot to the other ... from an outside edge to an outside edge.

1 Start by standing up tall with your feet together at 90 degrees – your left leg leading. Your left arm, hip and shoulder should be held forwards and your right arm, hip and shoulder held slightly backwards. Focus on something ahead of you and stay focused on that.

2 Bend your knees and, with the left side of your body leading, skate forwards onto the outside edge of your left skate. Extend your free leg (right) behind and turn out your foot.

3 Lower your free foot (right) and place the heel next to the instep of your skating foot.

4 Transfer your weight onto the outside edge of your right foot. Turn your hips, shoulders and upper body strongly to the left and allow your feet to turn. Keep them in the same position throughout the 180-degree rotation – turning cleanly from left to right.

8 Free skating

spirals • spins • jumps

Now that you can skate forwards and backwards and turn, you're ready to look at some of the moves, spins and jumps that are an important part of free skating.

Forward spiral

Although this one sounds like a spin, it isn't! It's a beautiful move that's similar to an arabesque in ballet. It's simplest to perform while moving forwards in a straight line, but can also be performed when travelling backwards, or on an edge.

1 To start, stand up tall. Make about four forward strokes.

2 Hold your arms out to the side to help you balance. Put your weight on your left leg while stretching forwards with your upper body and raising your free leg (the right one) behind you.

3 Extend your free leg behind you to at least hip-height and turn out your free foot and leg so that the blade is parallel to the ice. Keep your head raised and your shoulders back all the time. Hold for 10 counts.

There should be a curve from the top of your head to your skate.

Keep your head raised. Hold your arms at shoulder height.

Spins

Audiences love to see spins and, likewise, top skaters recognise the drama and excitement their multiple rotations provide. Because they demand such energy and athleticism, the spins are usually well-spaced within a programme.

Fastest spinners

Ronnie Robertson (1956 Olympic Silver Medalist) is believed to have been one of the fastest spinners in skating history. With his spins, he was said to be able to make 240 full rotations per minute!

One-footed teapot (or 'shoot the duck')

Although this move is rarely seen in free skating programmes, it's a useful one to learn. It introduces you to the position of the more advanced sit spin and it's an excellent balancing exercise.

1 To start, stand up tall. Take a few forward pushes to gather speed and glide forwards.

2 Extend both your arms forwards. Stand on your preferred foot and stretch your other leg (free leg) out in front of you, pointing your toes.

3 Bend your skating knee and lower yourself close to the ice surface. Meanwhile keep your free leg straight and in front of you and raised slightly off the ice.

4 Hold this position as long as you can. Stand up carefully by bringing your free foot next to your skating foot as you rise, and then standing on both feet.

THE TEAPOT/'DUCK' CHALLENGE

✽ Try waiting until you are upright before putting your free foot down on the ice!

Two-foot spin

Your first spin!

1 Start by standing tall, with your feet parallel and slightly apart and your knees bent, putting your weight slightly on your inside edges.

TO TURN TO THE LEFT (ANTI-CLOCKWISE)
2 Hold your left arm forwards at shoulder height and pull your right shoulder back with your arm outstretched.

3 Point your toes inwards slightly.

4 Push off with your right foot, bring your right arm and shoulder strongly forwards and turn your upper body to the left – all at the same time!

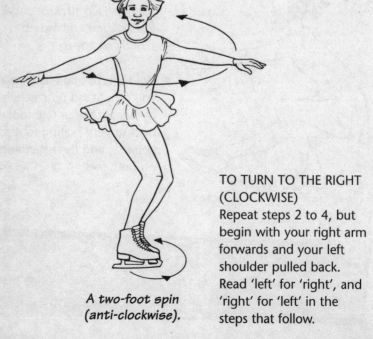

A two-foot spin (anti-clockwise).

TO TURN TO THE RIGHT (CLOCKWISE)
Repeat steps 2 to 4, but begin with your right arm forwards and your left shoulder pulled back. Read 'left' for 'right', and 'right' for 'left' in the steps that follow.

CUTTING EDGE
* Keep your shoulders level at all times.
* Keep your weight over the balls of your feet – but not on your toe-rakes.

The two-foot spin challenge

Decide which of these turning directions feels most comfortable to you. Practise spinning in that direction until you can complete three or more rotations (turns).

Arms!

While doing your turn, try making a circle with your arms in front of you (as if hugging someone) and quickly pull your arms to your chest.

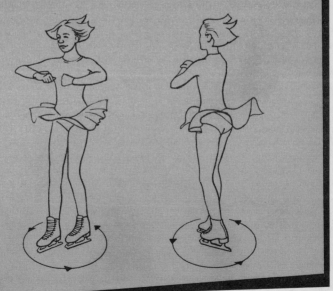

One-foot spin

Once you have mastered this important spin you'll be able to tackle more advanced spins with confidence.

1 In a clockwise direction, do a three-turn very quickly (see page 82). Straighten your skating knee to finish on the backward inside edge of your right skate while travelling backwards.

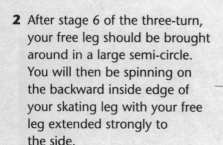

2 After stage 6 of the three-turn, your free leg should be brought around in a large semi-circle. You will then be spinning on the backward inside edge of your skating leg with your free leg extended strongly to the side.

3 Hold your arms out to your sides to steady yourself and carefully bend your extended free leg, placing your free foot next to your spinning knee.

4 As you spin in an anti-clockwise direction, make a circle with your arms in front of you (as if hugging someone) and quickly pull your hands and arms crossed into your chest with your elbows tucked in.

CUTTING EDGE
＊ Keep your shoulders and hips level while skating.
＊ Spin on the ball of your foot.
＊ Control that three-turn!
＊ Good expert coaching is essential.

A spin a-head of its time!

The Biellmann Spin is one in which both the skater's hands hold the free-leg skate above the head. This spin was named after the 1981 World Champion, Denise Biellmann (Switzerland), who first performed it. There is a statue of Biellmann and her spin inside the Vernet Sports Centre in Geneva, Switzerland – the site of the 1986 World Championships.

REMEMBER! Only attempt these spins under the guidance of an expert coach!

Longest spin

Natalie Krieg (Switzerland) holds the record for longest spin with one that lasted three minutes, twenty seconds.

Jumps

There are two groups of jumps in free skating:

✳ Edge jumps – where take-off is from an inside or an outside edge with no assistance from the toe-rake.

✳ Toe jumps – where the take-off is assisted by striking the toe-rake.

Power to the jump!

While the landings of most jumps look the same, the take-offs are often different. However, there is one thing for which all have a shared need ... and that is power! For all take-offs your weight must be over the take-off foot and your knee must bend deeply to give as much lift to your jump as possible.

... and the arms!

Before take-off, your arms should be extended and your shoulders level. As you begin to jump, let your arms drop. Next lift your arms to shoulder height to raise your upper body before pulling them in to the centre of your chest. Make sure your arms are controlled and level all the time.

In the air

From your head, down to your skating foot, your body
needs to be vertical while in the air to prevent you from
falling over.

Soft landings ... the usual landing position!

For most jumps you will land with a glide on a right back
outside (RBO) edge, with your right knee deeply bent and
your arms extended out to the sides.

CUTTING EDGE
* When taking off, don't lean forwards. When you land,
  hold your head up high.
* Have your arms at shoulder level when you land.
* Keep your shoulders down.

The bunny hop

The bunny hop has a forward take-off and no turns ...
a perfect first jump!

1 Start by standing
tall, then glide
forwards on your
left foot.

2 Swing your right
foot and your left
arm forwards while
springing off your
skating foot (left).

3 Land on the front
of your right skate –
your toe-rake – and
transfer your weight
immediately to the
forward outside
edge of your left
skate. Glide
forwards, swinging
your right arm as
you do so.

If you prefer to
take-off and land on
the opposite feet,
read 'right' for 'left'
and vice versa.

The three (or waltz) jump

Like the bunny hop, the three jump has a forward take-off, – with the addition of a half rotation (180 degrees) in the air and a backwards finish. It uses an outside edge at both take-off and landing. Perfect preparation for the Axel – an important advanced jump!

1 Start by standing tall, and with your knees bent, glide forwards on the outside edge of your left foot.

2 Pull your arms slightly behind your body. Spring from your left knee and press down on the front of your left blade, to jump over the toe-rake.

Meanwhile swing your right leg and both arms forwards and jump towards your left (anti-clockwise).

3 As you jump, cross your arms upwards in a relaxed position across your chest and keep your head held high.

The more you bend your knee, the higher your jump will be – within human limits!

100

4 Keeping your arms across your body, straighten your legs and keep them apart (as a star-jump).

5 Prepare to land (on your right leg) by opening your arms strongly out to your sides at shoulder height to slow you down. At the same time lift your left leg forwards and move your left arm forwards.

6 With your knee strongly bent, land on your right toe-rake. Skate backwards on an outside edge, swinging your free leg (left) gently to an extended position behind you. Hold this position.

The Axel jump

All single jumps – with the exception of the Axel and the three jump – begin with skater moving backwards and rotating up to once in the air before landing backwards. The Axel has a forward outside take-off and a back outside landing on the other foot – *one and a half turns* in the air!

The Salchow jump

Ten-times World Champion between 1900 and 1911, Ulrich
Salchow (Sweden) invented his own jump – the Salchow!
It is one of the six major jumps. It has a backwards take-off
from an inside edge and a backwards landing on an outside
edge – following one rotation in the air. The Salchow uses
the same starting position as the three/waltz jump, (you
must turn a three-turn to achieve the backward inside edge
before the take-off).

What are the other major jumps?

There are five other major jumps: the toe-loop, loop, flip,
Lutz and Axel.

EDGE JUMPS: THE SALCHOW, LOOP AND AXEL

* The Salchow and loop take off from a backward-moving
  edge.
* The Axel jump takes off from a forward outside edge
  (like the three/waltz jump that you practised).

TOE JUMPS: THE TOE-LOOP, FLIP AND LUTZ

* Toe jumps take-off from a backward moving edge. The
  lift comes from extending the free leg behind and
  pushing the toe-rake into the ice.

The flip jump

Who did it first?

Men's jumps successfully landed at national, World or Olympic competitions:

Quadruple Jump Combination
(quadruple toe-loop – double toe-loop)
(1991): Elvis Stojko (Canada)
Quadruple Jump (quadruple toe-loop)
(1988): Kurt Browning (Canada)
Triple Axel Combination
(triple Axel – double toe-loop)
(1985): Brian Orser (Canada)
Triple Axel (1978): Vern Taylor (Canada)
Triple Lutz (1962): Donald Jackson (Canada)
Triple Jump/Loop (1952): Dick Button (USA)
Double Axel (1948): Dick Button (USA)
*Double Lutz (1947): Dick Button (USA)
Loop (1910): Werner Rittberger (Germany) – the jump's inventor
Salchow (1909): Ulrich Salchow (Sweden)

* Single Lutz was created by Alois Lutz (Austria) who never competed in the World Championships.

AXEL JUMPS FROM FIGURE SKATING TO SPEED SKATING EVENTS!

Axel Paulsen (Norway) – the creator of the Axel jump – was a great speed skater. In 1882, Paulsen competed in his one and only International Figure Skating Competition. After this event in Vienna he returned to speed skating races for which he received prize money.

Who did it first?

Women's jumps successfully landed at national, World or Olympic competitions:

Triple Axel (1989): Midori Ito (Japan)
Triple Lutz (1987): Denise Biellmann (Switzerland)
Triple Salchow (1959): Jana Dočekalová (Czechoslovakia)
Double jump (a double Salchow) (1936): Cecilia College (GB)

* There is sometimes disagreement as to who successfully achieved the first jumps.

What a combination!

To really impress the judges, top skaters may perform a combination of up to four – or even five – jumps in a row. These are known as combination jumps.

Elvis Stojko

At the 1997 World Championships, Elvis Stojko was in fourth position at the end of the first programme. However, after landing a perfect quadruple-toe-triple toe combination – the first ever in the World Championships – he went on to win the Gold!

Figure skating

the art • the sport • competitions • the stars

Did you know?

Under the general term of 'figure skating' there are five separate competitions at International Level:

1 Men's figure skating
2 Ladies' figure skating
3 Ice dancing (see chapter 10)
4 Pairs skating (see chapter 11)
5 Synchronized skating (see chapter 12)

Figure skating – sport or art?

International figure skating today, with its graceful beauty and creativity, could be described by its audiences as a performing art. However, figure skating has been a competitive sport for over a hundred years.
Today competition skaters aim to:

1 Perform as difficult a routine as possible (technical merit).
2 Present the routine so that it looks its best (presentation).

Figure skating is forever making sporting leaps because it constantly offers new challenges, such as higher jumps and more rotations. With their amazing levels of fitness, agility and artistic talent, top skaters strive to be the world's best.

Figures of fun?

Tracing circles and figures of eight – using one foot at a time – used to be an essential part of competitive figure skating. Known as 'compulsory' or 'school' figures, top skaters had to learn about 69 in their careers, practising for over two hours each day. Sometimes a single figure contained three circles – all of which had to be performed as perfectly as possible for competitions. While some spectators claimed figures were boring to watch, others saw great value in them.

Compulsory figures were not popular with everyone.

Spotlight Janet Lynn (US)

During the early 1970s, Janet Lynn captivated everybody with her amazing free skating. Audiences and fellow skaters loved to watch her skate, but she never won the Gold – the figures that she struggled with carried half the marks! Audiences and skaters complained that the winners were rarely the most dazzling performers ...

More fabulous free skaters

Like Jackson Haines (USA) over a hundred years before them, Toller Cranston (Canada) and the late John Curry (UK) became known for their expressive movement and fabulous free skating. They both disliked skating figures.

John Curry

Toller Cranston

Had figures not been compulsory, both Curry's and Cranston's competition results would certainly have been consistently higher. While John's balletic style did go on to win him the Olympic Gold in 1976, Toller – who brought dramatic body positions spectacularly to the ice – never has. And yet, like Jackson Haines, he remains one of the greatest figure skating influences of our times.

The final figure in senior competitions ...

1968 Figures reduced from 60% to 50% of marks.

1987 Figures carried 20% of marks.

1988 I.S.U. decided to remove them from senior events.

1990 Figures made their last appearance at the 1990 World Championships.

Figure moves are still taught today to help teach good control of edges.

Figure skating competitions

Singles skating

Skaters are awarded marks out of six for each of the following sections:

1 **A Short Programme** which must last for 2 minutes and 40 seconds or less. There will be certain jumps, jump combinations, spins, steps and spin combinations that skaters must include in their short programmes. These are called 'required elements'. Judges award two marks – the first for the required elements; the second for presentation:

   Required elements: The movements the I.S.U. insists on being performed.

   Presentation: Judges want to see the skaters cover as much of the ice surface as possible, while skating elegantly and with originality. Skaters should be in time with the music and present a performance that is in keeping with it.

2 **Long Free Skating Programme:** the length of this programme depends on whether the skater is senior, junior, male or female – for men it is four and a half minutes; for ladies it is four minutes; for juniors it is less. There are no set moves so skaters try to show what they do best! Jumps can only be repeated if they are used in a combination second time around. Judges award one mark for technical merit and one for presentation:

   Technical merit: Judges look at how difficult the moves are. Good technique is essential: the take-offs and landings must be good; the height and length of jumps is important; the spins and footwork are looked at carefully.

   Presentation: As before, but judges also consider the skater's interpretation of the music.

10 | Ice dancing

clubs • leagues • competitions • the stars

Ice dancing and pairs skating

Ice dancing is a popular recreational sport as well as a major focal point of international competitions. Like competition-level pairs skating, it is elegant and dazzling, but it does not have the jumps, the overhead lifts or extended spins. Ice dancing has different rules and a greater emphasis on the way people move to the music.

Ice dance skates

Ice dancers wear skates that are slightly different to those of other skaters. The boots are softer and flexible for ease of movement. The blades are short at the back and usually thinner than figure skate blades – making the edges closer together.

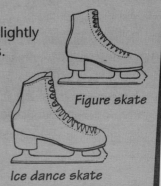

Figure skate

Ice dance skate

Dance Intervals

If you are interested in ice dancing look out for the dance intervals in public sessions. The dance interval is usually a 15-minute period when the disco music and special-effect lighting may be turned off and non-dancers take a break while the dancers perform the tango, waltz and foxtrot! As a beginner, it is fun to watch all the different styles of dancing that may be in full swing! If you're inspired you could then make enquiries about ice dance classes!

Did you know?

There are over 150 known ice dances. For some you only need to be able to skate forwards, while the most difficult dances require you to be a very experienced skater.

The waltz hold

The kilian hold

The ice dance challenge

Once you have learnt to skate a number of the moves outlined in this book, ice dancing will present you with a new and sociable challenge. From learning dance moves – to learning to work with a partner in time to music – a whole new world opens up!

Ice dance clubs

Look out at your local rink for 'Learn to dance' classes. Once you have learnt a few basic moves you could meet up with other interested people by joining the Ice Dance Club.

Find out the name of the club secretary and check with them the club's entry requirements before you join. For some you will simply need basic skating skills, while for others you may have to have reached a certain standard – and possibly have some knowledge of the easiest dances.

The Ice Dance League

As a Club member, and with a few dances under your belt, you will be able to enjoy many social events. It's a great way to meet up with skaters – of all abilities and ages – with a common interest. And, after some practice, you may decide to enter club and inter-club competitions such as those run by the Ice Dance League.

Ice dance competitions

There are three parts to competitions:

Compulsory dance

Skaters perform a set sequence of ice dance moves to ballroom or Latin music. Judges award two marks each: one for technique and one for timing and expression.
They look for:

* Good edge work.
* Unison – skaters must keep good time with each other.
* Musical timing.
* Correct patterns being formed on the ice in the correct areas.

Original dance

Competitors create and present their own dance routine to a set piece of music: maybe a quickstep, tango, jive, *paso doble*, Latin or waltz. Judges award two sets of marks for:

* **Composition** – the way the moves are put together.
* **Presentation** – the delivery of the routine.

Free dance

Having chosen their own theme and music, competitors present their own, free dance routine. Judges award one mark each for:

* **Technical merit** – keeping time to music and to each other, speed, clever footwork, well-performed lifts and good use of the ice surface – to deliver as difficult a routine as possible.
* **Presentation** – to perform the routine to its best visual effect, interpreting music with an original and well-constructed programme of moves.

Jayne Torvill and Christopher Dean (UK)

Between each of the World Ice Dance Championships from 1981 to 1984 that Jane Torvill and Christopher Dean won, they rarely received a mark that wasn't perfect. They have even received a few perfect scores for technical excellence – a very rare event in skating history. 'Bolero', their programme that won them Gold Medals at both the 1984 Winter Olympics and the 1984 World Championships Free Dance competitions, is now legendary.

One of Torvill and Dean's great strengths was their (and particularly Dean's) great imagination. They created exciting new moves and worked them ingeniously around the I.S.U.'s rules. For the judges trying to work out whether they had stayed within the I.S.U.'s guidelines, it was rather like untangling an intricate puzzle ...

If ice dancers were only allowed to rotate one and a half times, Torvill and Dean would do four! But – because they cleverly combined the rotations with other moves – the rotations weren't continuous and the judges couldn't complain! The audiences were in raptures; ice dancing was made popular and the I.S.U. were left to hastily rewrite the rules!

➤

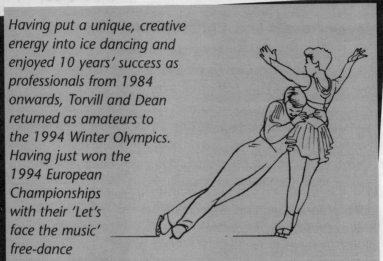

Having put a unique, creative energy into ice dancing and enjoyed 10 years' success as professionals from 1984 onwards, Torvill and Dean returned as amateurs to the 1994 Winter Olympics. Having just won the 1994 European Championships with their 'Let's face the music' free-dance programme, Jayne Torvill and Christopher Dean were disappointed to be awarded the Olympic Bronze. Their programme wasn't possibly as daring as 'Bolero' had been, but many moves for which they had won praise in 1984 were no longer allowed by the I.S.U.

Record breaker

Ludmila Pakhmova and Alexandr Gorshkov (her husband) won six World Ice Dance titles in 1970 to 74 and 1976. In 1976, they also won the first Olympic Ice Dance title.

11 Pairs skating

the programmes and competitions • the stars

Is pairs skating the same as ice dancing?

Ice dancing includes some pairs skating, but pairs skating also has a lot more. If you combine elements of ice dancing, compulsory dances and free skating; include overhead lifts, throws and spins; add greater speed and danger ... there you have the basics of pairs skating! Pairs skating is spectacular to watch, but is no sport for the faint-hearted! As well as needing the thorough training of a specialist coach, you'll need to be an excellent free skater to try it! Training is very rigorous.

It is important for pairs partners to be of a similar standard and age. The man in particular needs to be very strong to lift and spin his partner. Like ice dancing, skating in unison (in time with each other) is essential – otherwise it can be disastrous.

Pairs competitions

For most of us mere mortals, the closest we will come to pairs skating competitions is possibly the television (but please feel free to prove me wrong!) There are two programmes in competitive pairs skating:

1 Short Programme

Skaters have to perform certain lifts, pair spins and a thrown jump. The programme must also include certain solo jumps, spins and step sequences. Judges award one mark each for:

* **Required elements** – the moves the I.S.U. insists on being performed.

* **Presentation.**

2 Long Programme

For seniors, the long programme lasts four and a half minutes; for juniors it lasts four minutes. Above all, pairs try to skate gracefully and in time with each other during this time. They must skate with speed, using edges well, while covering as much of the ice's surface as possible. The technical skills (see below) are also important. Judges award one mark each for:

* **Technical merit** – the difficulty level of the lifts, throws and pair spins, plus solo jumps and spins – and how well everything is performed.

* **Presentation.**

Spotlight

During the 1960s, Ludmila Belousova and Oleg Protopopov turned around the world of pair skating with their artistic style and creation of new versions of old moves. One such move was the 'death spiral' that features in pair skating programmes today. Rather than perform this on the outside edge, they performed the 'death spiral' on an inside edge.

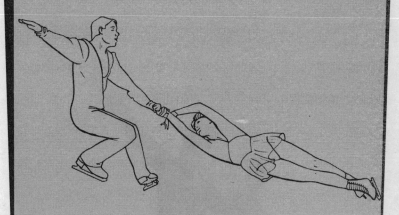

In 1965, Oleg Protopopov and Ludmila Belousova won the first of what was to be four World Championship Gold Medals in succession. This was the start of the Soviet Union winning the Pairs at the World Championships for fourteen years in a row. To this day Soviet/former-Soviet pairs have won nearly every championship since.

Record breaker

Highest number of pairs titles.

Soviet skater Irina Rodnina won 10 World Pairs titles in a row! Between 1969 and 1972 she won four with Alexei Ulanov, and from 1973 to 1978 she won six with her husband Alexandr Zaitsev. This completed the unbroken, fourteen-year Soviet 'reign' of the World's Pairs that had begun with Ludmila Belousova and Oleg Protopopov.

More ice skating options

speed skating • ice hockey • synchronization

Speed skating

Speed skating – sometimes known as power skating – is one of the fastest and most exciting sports on two legs. It has two forms:

* **Long track speed skating** – takes place on large indoor and outdoor tracks with skaters racing against the clock.

* **Short track speed skating** – skaters race against each other around a very tight indoor track. There are separate events for men's, women's and junior competitions, as well as for relays.

Speed skaters wear skin-tight, go-fast suits made from lightweight, stretchy fabric. They also wear specially designed speed skates.
Turn to pages 28-29 for more information on speed skating.

Ice hockey

A game of ice hockey lasts 60 minutes. The match is divided into three 20-minute intervals, during which time the two teams chase the puck to try to score goals. Can you remember what the puck is made from?*

A team is made up of six players – one of whom is the goal-minder. (He's the one in goal with the special face-mask, additional leg-guards, chest protector and even thicker gloves than the other players!) Like the other players, the goal-minder has a special wooden ice hockey stick and the standard protective clothing: a helmet, knee- and elbow-pads, and shoulder- and shin-guards too. As with any team sport, the rules are clear ... break any and you could spend two minutes or more in the penalty box!

*Turn to page 26 or the glossary on pages 124-125 for the answer.

Synchronized Skating

A synchronized skating team may have between 12 and 24 skaters who perform highly practised group moves to music. Aiming for perfect unison (togetherness), each skater must skate with great accuracy, perfectly in time with the rest of the team.

Many rinks now have synchronized skating teams. If you would like to join one you will need to have:
* ambition to be an excellent team member.
* lots of time to practise regularly with the team.
* a similar skating ability to the other team members.
* a good sense of rhythm and timing to music.
* an ability to learn steps and sequences quickly.
* the same height as the other team members.

It's a challenge but, as with other forms of ice skating, think of the fun you could have and all the friendships you might make!

CUTTING EDGE
* Synchronized skating was previously called 'precision skating'.

121

Want to know more?

useful addresses • more information • websites

Useful worldwide addresses for news about ice skating

Australian Amateur Ice Racing Council Inc.
5 First Avenue, Epping, NSW 2121
Tel: (00) 612 9673 1929

Australian Professional Skaters Association (APSA)
2 Queen Street, Croydon,
NSW 2132
Tel: (00) 612 9798 9008
E-mail:
ssecured@nsw.bigpond.net.au
Website: **www.apsa.one.net.au**
The Association was set up to improve the standard of coaching and amateur skating in Australia. Together with Ice Skating Australia Inc., the APSA runs coaching courses across Australia.

Canadian Figure Skating Association (CFSA)
1600 James Naismith Drive,
Gloucester, Ontario K1B 5N4
Tel: (001) 613 747 1007
E-mail: cfsa@cfsa.ca
Website: **www.cfsa.ca**

Ice Hockey UK
The Galleries of Justice, Shire Hall, High Pavement, The Lace Market, Nottingham NG1 1HN
Tel: 0115 915 9204
E-mail:
hockey@ukhockey.freeserve.co.uk
Website:
www.icehockeyuk.co.uk

Ice Skating Australia (ISA) Inc.
PO Box 567, Archerfield,
Queensland 4108
Tel: (00) 617 3277 4618
E-mail: administration@isa.org.au
Websites:
www.skatingaus.com.au and
www.isa.org.au
Formerly the National Ice Skating Association of Australia, ISA can provide more information on:
❀ Australian figure skating.
❀ 'Aussie Skate Program'.
❀ Ice skating rinks in Australia.
❀ Other skating associations.
❀ Forthcoming skating events.

International Skating Union (ISU)
Chemin de Primerose 2,
CH-1007 Lausanne, Switzerland
Tel: (+41) 21 612 6666
E-mail: info@isu.ch
Website: **www.isu.org**

For more information about:
- Figure skating.
- Synchronized skating.
- Short track speed skating.
- International ice skating events (past and future).

The National Coaching Foundation
114 Cardigan Road, Headingley, Leeds LS6 3BJ
Tel: 0113 274 4802
E-mail: coaching@ncs.org.uk
Website: **www.ncs.org.uk**
If your aim is to become a coach, look no further! The foundation can offer plenty of advice and provide you with a list of useful contacts. Members receive their magazine – *Faster, Higher, Stronger*.

National Ice Skating Association (NISA) of UK Ltd
First Floor, 114-116 Curtain Road, London EC2A 3AH
Tel: 0207 613 1188
Fax: 0207 613 4616
E-mail: Nisa@iceskating.co.uk
Website: **www.iceskating.org.uk**
For more information about:
- Figure skating.
- Short track speed skating (no UK long track speed skating).
- Synchronized skating.
- Recreational skating.
- FUN SKATE learn-to-skate scheme.
- Ice rinks in UK.
- *Ice Link* magazine – the newspaper of the NISA UK

Additional websites

Check out these sites and keep a look-out for useful links to other skating sites.

http://frog.simplenet.com/skateweb/
The figure skating page.

www.eiha.co.uk
The English Ice Hockey Association site.

www.figureskating.com
Find out about the Olympic and World Championship results of years gone by.

www.iceweb.co.uk
The Ice Hockey Superleague page.

www.web4.sportsline.com
For the latest news on ice sports.

www.nswisa.com
The website for the New South Wales Ice Skating Association, Australia.

Magazines

Blades on Ice (USA)
www.bladesonice.com

International Figure Skating (USA)
www.ifsmagazine.com

Skater's Edge
A unique figure-skating magazine. Each issue contains detailed instructional articles, step-by-step photos, illustrated skating tips and much more.

Glossary

absorbent skateguards Guards made from soft, absorbent fabric to keep skates/blades dry and rust-free.

Axel jump The jump invented by Axel Paulsen (Norway). The skater takes off from a forward outside edge on the skating foot, makes one and a half mid-air turns and lands on the back outside edge of the other foot.

blade/skate guards Solid rubber or plastic protective covers that are placed over blades when wearing skates off ice.

camel spin A spin in the arabesque position on the flat of the blade. Created by Jackson Haines.

combination jumps A series of jumps where the end of one jump becomes the start of the next.

compulsory (school) figures Tracing on the ice of figures of eight, three-circle figures and other loops.

crossover A forward or backward movement where one foot crosses over the other to create a gradual turning movement.

death spiral A move in pairs skating in which the man pivots on the spot with his knees bent while holding his partner's hand. His partner circles around him in an almost horizontal position just above the ice on an edge.

dip Bending both knees and lowering the body down towards the ice in a balanced and upright position.

edge The side of the blade that cuts into the ice and creates the curve

on the ice. Curves vary depending on the position and angle.

edge jump A jump where the take-off is from an inside or outside edge – without a toe-strike.

English style Style of skating that began at the end of the 18th century (and is still practised at one rink today). Skaters kept an elegant, upright posture, while tracing figures on the ice. The same position was held until a change of edge.

figures Tracings made on the ice in specific patterns.

figure skating 1750-1990: tracing set patterns or figures on ice. Since 1990: 'free skating'.

Flip jump A Salchow jump with a toe-strike (from the toe-rake).

free foot/leg The non-skating foot/leg.

glide A continuous movement (forwards or backwards) on one foot.

grind The hollow along the blade's length between the two edges.

inside edge The edge on the inner side of the skating foot.

International style The style of most figure skating today.

lift A move in pairs skating in which the man lifts his partner above his head, extending one or both of his arms.

loop jump A jump with one rotation in the air. Take-off is from a backward outside edge – sometimes with a toe-strike from the toe-rake (toe-pick). Landing is on the same foot as the take-off.

Lutz jump The jump invented by Alois Lutz (Austria). An anti-clockwise jump that is performed after a gliding movement in a clockwise direction. Take-off is assisted by using the toe-rake of the free foot together with the back outside edge of the skating foot. The landing is on the back outside edge of the opposite foot (free foot).

mohawk A 180-degree turn from forwards to backwards, from one foot to the other on the same edges.

outside edge The edge on the outer side of the skating foot.

pattern An impression or image made on the ice.

presentation Competition judges consider the visual effect of the skating programme, the interpretation of the music and the way the moves are put together.

puck The special rubber disc used in ice hockey.

pushing foot The non-skating foot whose edges the skater uses to press into the ice. With this foot firmly on the ice, the skater is able to push off from it onto the skating foot.

radius (or rocker) The curve that runs from the toe to the heel of the blade.

required elements The moves the I.S.U. insists on being performed in competitions.

revolution A 360-degree turn.

rotation A full 360-degree turn.

Salchow A jump invented by Ulrich Salchow (Sweden). The skater takes off from the back inside edge of the skating foot, makes a full mid-air turn and lands on the back outside edge of the opposite foot.

sit spin Spin (invented by Jackson Haines): the skating knee is bent, the skater almost sitting, and the free leg is extended forwards.

skating foot/leg The foot/leg that is on the ice.

spinning knee The knee of skating leg that supports the body in a spin.

spiral Position (with many variations) in which the free leg is extended and raised high behind the skating leg, like an arabesque in ballet.

spread eagle A move where one foot is on a forward edge and one foot is on a backward edge, with the feet turned out at 180 degrees.

stroke The flowing movement of pushing off from one skate to glide on the other.

technical merit Competition judges consider the level of difficulty of the moves and award marks for how well the moves are performed.

three-turn A turn (from either forwards or backwards) of 180 degrees on one foot, which traces a number three.

toe jump A toe-strike jump with take-off from the toe-rake (toe-pick).

toe-loop jump A jump from a backward moving edge with a toe-strike.

toe-rake (toe-pick) The sharp, jagged section at the front of the blade used for jumps and spins and special toe steps.

unison Keeping good timing of movement with others during a performance.

'V'-position Starting position with heels together and toes pointed outwards.

Index

super.activ

0 340 773294	Acting	£3.99	☐
0 340 764686	Athletics	£3.99	☐
0 340 791578	Basketball	£3.99	☐
0 340 791535	Cartooning	£3.99	☐
0 340 791624	Chess	£3.99	☐
0 340 791586	Computers Unlimited	£3.99	☐
0 340 79156X	Cricket	£3.99	☐
0 340 791594	Drawing	£3.99	☐
0 340 791632	Film-making	£3.99	☐
0 340 791675	Fishing	£3.99	☐
0 340 791519	Football	£3.99	☐
0 340 76466X	Golf	£3.99	☐
0 340 778970	Gymnastics	£3.99	☐
0 340 791527	In-line Skating	£3.99	☐
0 340 764678	Juggling	£3.99	☐
0 340 749504	Karate	£3.99	☐
0 340 791640	The Internet	£3.99	☐
0 340 791683	Memory Workout	£3.99	☐
0 340 736283	Pop Music	£3.99	☐
0 340 791551	Riding	£3.99	☐
0 340 764694	Room Makeover	£3.99	☐
0 340 791659	Rugby	£3.99	☐
0 340 791608	Skateboarding	£3.99	☐
0 340 791667	Snowboarding	£3.99	☐
0 340 791616	Swimming	£3.99	☐
0 340 764465	Tennis	£3.99	☐
0 340 773332	Writing	£3.99	☐
0 340 784822	Your Own Chat Room	£3.99	☐
0 340 791543	Your Own Website	£3.99	☐

ORDER FORM

Books in the superactiv series are available at your local bookshop, or can be ordered direct from the publisher. A complete list of titles is given on the previous page. Just tick the titles you would like and complete the details below. Prices and availability are subject to change without prior notice.

Please enclose a cheque or postal order made payable to Bookpoint Ltd, and send to: Hodder Children's Books, Cash Sales Dept, Bookpoint, 39 Milton Park, Abingdon, Oxon OX14 4TD. Email address: orders@bookpoint.co.uk.

If you would prefer to pay by credit card, our call centre team would be delighted to take your order by telephone. Our direct line is 01235 400414 (lines open 9.00 am – 6.00 pm, Monday to Saturday; 24-hour message answering service). Alternatively you can send a fax on 01235 400454.

Title .... First name .... Surname ....

Address ....

....

....

Daytime tel .... Postcode...................................

If you would prefer to post a credit card order, please complete the following.

Please debit my Visa/Access/Diner's Card/American Express (delete as applicable) card number:

Signature ....Expiry Date ....

If you would NOT like to receive further information on our products, please tick ☐ .